Life in the
COMBAT
ZONE

HOW TO SURVIVE, THRIVE, AND OVERCOME
IN THE MIDST OF DIFFICULT SITUATIONS

RICK RENNER

Life in the Combat Zone:
How To Survive, Thrive, and Overcome
   in the Midst of Difficult Situations
ISBN: 978-1-68031-213-3

Published by Harrison House Publishers
Tulsa, OK 74145
www.harrisonhouse.com

5th Printing

Editorial Consultants: Cynthia D. Hansen and Rebecca L. Gilbert
Text Design/Layout: Lisa Simpson, www.SimpsonProductions.net
Cover and Graphic Design: Debbie Pullman,
   Zoe Life Creative Media
   Design@ZoeLifeCreative.com, www.ZoeLifeCreative.com

ENDORSEMENTS

Dr. Rick Renner's ministry of preaching, teaching, and writing is characterized by faithfulness; therefore, God has uniquely qualified him to bless the Church with *Life in the Combat Zone*. Let Dr. Renner's electrifying book challenge you to stay committed and lavish you with encouragement to "be strong in the Lord and the power of His might"! Although Dr. Renner is known the world over as a scholar and statesman, his true anointing is revealed with his keen ability to make profound biblical truths applicable to daily life. Whether you are a busy mom or a discouraged pastor, whether you are walking the lonely road of leadership or just setting out in your Christian walk — *Life in the Combat Zone* is a book you will treasure not only with your first read, but again and again as you study its rich contents to grow in the grace and knowledge of Jesus Christ.

Jeremiah J. Johnston, Ph.D.
President
Christian Thinkers Society

I just finished *Life in the Combat Zone*. I feel like I have been to boot camp, and I am ready and equipped for battle! What an amazing study. It makes me want to teach it to my church from cover to cover. In this spiritual climate we live in, it is absolutely necessary to know how to stand and win. Rick Renner has created a thorough and detailed study uncovering the devil's strategies and how to overcome them. He has also clearly defined the role of the Church and how God promotes in His Kingdom. As a pastor, I have mined some golden nuggets that I will be passing along to my congregation. Once again, thank you, Rick, for the clarity with which you communicate and your heart for every believer to succeed. Thank you for helping us all to "survive, thrive, and overcome in the midst of difficult situations."

George Pearsons
Senior Pastor
Eagle Mountain International Church
CEO, Kenneth Copeland Ministries

I have known Rick Renner for many years and hold him in high regard as a teacher of the Word. I personally consider Rick to be a modern-day layman's theologian. His understanding and interpretation of the Greek allows readers to have fresh insight into the Word of God that challenges every believer. His consistent excellence in ministry has blessed many around the world. *Life in the Combat Zone* contains a wealth of knowledge that I believe will enable all Christians to learn how to deal with difficult situations and overcome adversity. Readers will appreciate the extent of research and extreme care taken to educate us to boldly challenge the kingdom of darkness, storm the gates of hell, and become a champion for His cause. This book supports my life motto: *I cannot be defeated and I will not quit!*

> *Kenneth W. Hagin*
> President, Kenneth Hagin Ministries
> Pastor, RHEMA Bible Church
> President, RHEMA Bible Training
> College

Not only is Rick a rigorous scholar and dear friend, but he is also filled with wisdom. Any information he gives in his books and on the platform is life-changing. I have had many long, deep, and fascinating discussions with him, and I am always so inspired and learn so much from him. This book is a blessing and *well* worth the investment of your time.

> *Dr. Caroline Leaf*
> Cognitive Neuroscientist and
> Communication Pathologist
> Author and Speaker

Who can write better and give clearer revelation than Rick Renner? Always I have found Rick's writings to work where I really live. *Life in the Combat Zone* opens up new arenas of faith for us to walk in no matter what realm of life we live in. I love this new book — it hits where the rubber meets the road. God bless you, Rick Renner! I appreciate you to no end.

> *Dr. Marilyn Hickey*
> President and Founder
> Marilyn Hickey Ministries

Life in the Combat Zone is an imperative read for today's believers. When I think of Rick's ministry, the primary word that comes to mind is "rich," and this book is no exception. It is rich in biblical content, rich in historical context, and rich in practical application. In these pages, you will gain profound insight about the strategies of our spiritual enemy. But even more importantly, you will discover the powerful and inexhaustible supply of God's resources that are available to you. If you desire to be an overcomer, I know of no better resource to recommend than *Life in the Combat Zone*.

Tony Cooke
Author and Bible Teacher

Rick Renner has done it again — a masterpiece written with his classic expertise. Rick is not only an excellent writer, but he also always produces evidence and legitimate history to support his topic. I am a former U.S. Marine Vietnam veteran and Marine instructor. This book is filled with truths and principles that have been proven spiritually, naturally, and even militarily. The Holy Spirit told me that this book will change many lives forever. I pray you are one of those. Job well done, Rick!

Mark T. Barclay
Preacher of Righteousness

In his newest book, *Life in the Combat Zone*, Rick Renner has given us a powerful, practical, and scholarly "field guide" to thrive and survive in the midst of difficult situations. His rich understanding of the times, of the Church, of history, and of the Greek language come together and make this a compelling must-read for the days in which we live. I heartily recommend Rick's book for every Christian who wants to step up as a good soldier of Jesus Christ and for every leader called to guide troops in the combat zone!

Beth Jones
Pastor/Author
Valley Family Church/The Basics
With Beth

God's words that He chose to use in the original texts of the Bible hold treasure troves of meaning that I hold precious. Hebrew I have studied, and I'm just a learner, not an expert. But in the Greek of the New Testament, and particularly in the oh-so-important letters written to the Body of Christ, Rick Renner's in-depth study and revelation causes greater light of God's meaning to shine into my spirit and soul. The Bible says we are to be overcomers. Never is there a hint that we are to *be* overcome. Yet the very term "overcomers" hints that there is something *to* overcome. This book will open to you God's message of victory, when circumstances may seem to say otherwise.

Dr. Billye Brim
President, Prayer Mountain
in the Ozarks

Rick Renner has written another amazing book that will help you thrive in life instead of simply *survive* life. *Life in the Combat Zone* explains in depth what character qualities believers must cultivate to overcome in every arena of life. This book will encourage you to stay in the fight of faith, no matter what opposition you might face, and to never, ever give up!

Lisa Osteen Comes
Associate Pastor, Lakewood Church
Author, *You Are Made for More!*

We truly live on the frontlines of the battles of life. Rick Renner has nailed this in his book *Life in the Combat Zone*. From so many scriptures, Rick lets us know the victory Jesus left us at His resurrection. You will finish each chapter stronger and better prepared to see your problems fall before you. And when you finish the book, you will want to share it with your Christian friends. We owe Rick Renner a debt of gratitude for this book.

Pastor Bob Yandian
Author and Bible Teacher

Life in the Combat Zone is where many of us are permanently stationed on divine assignment from God. So how do we fend off the daily barrage of demonic attacks? Rick Renner's new book is filled with invaluable intelligence, especially when it comes to fighting the adversary's underhanded fear tactics. This book will encourage you to stay at your post, complete your mission, stand your ground, and give no place to the enemy. Spiritual warfare is *real* — so welcome to the front lines!

David Crank
Senior Pastor, FaithChurch.com,
St. Louis and West Palm Beach
Author, *Solving Your Money Problems*

Few people have impacted my life and ministry the way Rick Renner has through his books and his teaching. *Life in the Combat Zone* is sure to have the same impact on you, your family, your business, and your ministry. Whether you realize it or not, at this very moment you are engaged in a fight for your life — but be encouraged, knowing that you will find your clear path to victory in the pages of this book.

Jeremy Pearsons
Pearsons Ministries International

Rick Renner's new book is so important for the Church in this hour. It's time to awaken the Body of Christ for the spiritual battle that we as believers are called to fight. I've always loved Rick's books, and I know this one will impact anyone who reads it!

Paul Daugherty
Pastor, Victory Christian Center
Tulsa, OK

DEDICATION

This book is dedicated to that faithful group of soldiers who have stood alongside us in our ministry over the years for many decades. Without these faithful warriors at our sides, it would have been impossible to achieve the victories we've seen accomplished in the course of our ministry. On that day when we stand before the Judgment Seat of Christ to give account for what we did with our lives and ministry, I know that this group of faithful soldiers will be rewarded for their sacrificial service to Christ and covenant commitment to us. I am eternally grateful, and I dedicate this book to them.

CONTENTS

CHAPTER ONE

THE FRONT LINES OF BATTLE

*L*iving life on the front lines of battle can be exciting! *If you score a big victory there, you will be heralded as one of God's champions.* However, the front lines are also where the greatest number of attacks occurs. Out on the front lines — the cutting edge — Satan hits hard and often, trying to drive back the Lord's brave soldiers who are storming hell's gates and taking new ground for His Kingdom. And as the end of this age approaches, the severity of these attacks is becoming more acute.

I can personally testify to many satanic attacks that have come against my family and me as we have pressed forward to take new territory for the Kingdom of God over the years. The enemy is always looking for ways to sabotage the life of a true front-line soldier. Therefore, in order to stand our ground and fight, *we as believers have to live lives that leave no doors open to the enemy.*

> **In order to stand our ground and fight,** *we as believers have to live lives that leave no doors open to the enemy.*

If an unprepared believer is hit hard by one of Satan's attacks, it has the potential of removing him or her permanently from the fight. History has shown time and time again that some believers are unwilling to do what is necessary to withstand the enemy's onslaughts. Instead of standing their ground and tenaciously fighting back, they crumble under the pressure and retreat — abandoning their brothers and sisters in Christ to fight the battle on their own. Often these defectors are fearful that they'll be associated with "radicals" who might fail or become objects of ridicule or scorn. As a result, they secede the front lines of battle that God has called them to protect. This, of course, is exactly what Satan wants them to do.

There is no doubt about it — living in the combat zone requires courage and wisdom! You must possess fierce determination and be able to understand the devil's strategies so you can overcome his attacks and move forward to win fresh victories and take new territory for the Kingdom of God.

God is calling! He is looking for a special brand of believers who want to enter the combat zone and live there according to His will and His ways. He needs resolute, committed Christians who know their place of victory in Christ and will challenge the devil, storm the gates of hell, and remain faithful until the job is accomplished. God is seeking spiritual warriors who will step forward to be enlisted ahead of the rest of the ranks, ready to fearlessly look the enemy in the eye and do battle!

Although the risks are certain, they are far outweighed by the great rewards — *and* the far-reaching consequences of choosing *not* to fight. Warriors who avoid the battle stand to lose out on rewards, both in this life and the next. But for those who refuse to leave their position on the front lines until the battle is over, these brave spiritual warriors will have the "first pick" of the enemy's plunder!

YOU HAVE ENTERED THE COMBAT ZONE!

When the apostle Paul wrote his first epistle to Timothy, things were going wonderfully in the church of Ephesus where the younger minister was pastor. This was the leading congregation of all the churches in the Roman province of Asia (the western portion of modern-day Turkey). At that time, the church had been experiencing incredible, supernatural growth at a spectacular rate. In fact, Timothy's church was growing so fast that he didn't even know how to organize his congregation. So he wrote to Paul, asking advice about how to cope with the various issues connected with a rapidly expanding church.

So we see that the book of First Timothy is a letter of instruction and counsel written to a church in its prime. However, when we read Second Timothy, it is evident that the picture is very different and that the church of Ephesus wasn't doing well at all. In the three years that had transpired between Paul's first and second epistles to Timothy, the Ephesian church's situation had radically changed. During those interim years, circumstances had definitely taken a turn for the worse for this congregation, and Timothy had become fretful and worried.

A landmark event had occurred that shook the Early Church to its core and caused many believers to reassess their commitment to the faith. Timothy was confronting scandal, defection, lies, betrayal, and persecution. Instead of leading a flourishing church, Timothy found himself leading a dramatically shrinking congregation. But that was only the beginning of this younger minister's problems! Timothy was not only battling anxiety over the declining condition of his church, but he was also deeply afraid of the very real possibility that he might be *martyred*.

Timothy had suddenly found himself right in the middle of the combat zone!

In certain ways, Timothy's predicament was similar to struggles that many in the Church face today. Over recent years, Christians and unbelievers alike have been repeatedly shocked as high-profile believers who were once white-hot for Jesus began to compromise their faith and make concessions with the lost world around them.

In addition, many Christians have become caught up in a convenience-obsessed mindset that shuns dedication and hard work. Instead, they have gravitated toward seeker-friendly atmospheres where increasingly diluted versions of the Bible are taught. Churches have popped up everywhere, often filled with believers who have a shallow, surface knowledge of the Bible at best. At worst, many don't believe the Bible is God's infallible Word *or* that Jesus is the only way to Heaven and to God. Steadfast men and women of God who have held to a stricter view of Scripture have begun to find themselves on the fringes of a Church that is becoming increasingly unfamiliar with the foundational teachings of God's Word.

> **Every day the battle intensifies for souls and sound doctrine. The stark reality of warfare and confrontation has been forced upon us, and we *must* fight back, whether we like it or not.**

In modern history, times have changed for consecrated and dedicated believers, especially over the past few decades. Every day the battle intensifies for souls and sound doctrine. Every day the struggle seems greater to obtain the needed finances to spread the Gospel and sustain the survival of solid, Bible-believing local churches. The stark reality of warfare and confrontation has been forced upon us, and we *must* fight back, whether we like it or not.

The Cause of Timothy's Troubles

However, before we further discuss our own lives in the combat zone, let's look at the event that unexpectedly thrust Timothy on to the front lines of an intense spiritual battle.

As Timothy was overseeing a prosperous and rapidly growing church in Ephesus, Nero was nearing the end of his reign as emperor of the Roman Empire. Within a short time, the emperor would instigate the first large-scale brutal persecution of the Church. This period of persecution would not only be devastating to the Church at the time, but it would also lay the foundation for the next few centuries of intermittent vicious persecution that plagued believers until the eventual collapse of Roman paganism in the Fourth Century AD.

On the surface, Nero's early years as emperor were generally looked upon in a favorable light. He spearheaded many programs that appealed to the lower classes; he initiated large, public-construction projects; and he appealed to the Senate by offering them more autonomy.

However, this stability didn't last long. Nero's ascension to the throne had been embroiled in conspiracy and scandal, and as a result, he felt the need to take measures that would consolidate his power and quash any who might deny his claim to the throne. As the years progressed, Nero became consumed with lust for power and increasingly paranoid about subversion. Consequently, his attempts to cement his hold on the throne degenerated into a campaign of bloodshed and fear against any whom he perceived to be a threat to his rule.

Nero's calculated purging of his ranks would claim the lives of many of Rome's elite, including multiple senators and Roman knights, his own mother, his first wife, his stepbrother, his tutor

Seneca, and even his pregnant second wife. As time passed, Nero began to act more like a beast than a man.

As Nero devolved into a cruel and brutal tyrant, his behavior simultaneously grew more ostentatious and erratic. He had always been known for his vanity and arrogance, but in the latter years of his reign, these character traits were magnified to an extraordinary degree. In fact, it is said Nero grew so deluded that he even began to lavish divine honors upon himself and to view himself as a god. His most infamous acts of insanity, though, began with the Great Fire of Rome in 64 AD.

THE GREAT FIRE OF ROME

Although there are always scholars to debate the facts, notable early historians report that Nero ordered his servants to set fire to the city of Rome to clear the way for him to construct a new palace. If this account is true, as is widely believed, his servants were dispatched throughout Rome with torches to set this diabolical scheme in action. The resultant fire spread quickly and soon grew to epic proportions. In fact, the renowned Roman statesman Tacitus recorded that the fire raged for 6 days and ravaged 10 of Rome's 14 major districts.[1]

The great inferno badly damaged many of Rome's beautiful, ornate monuments and structures. But the most dire and immediate consequence of the disaster was the great number of people who were left homeless and destitute. Rome had a huge population, and a large number of its residents were poor peasants and slaves who lived in little wooden shanties. These small shacks were extremely flammable, so when the blaze drew near, they were quickly and utterly consumed.

---

[1] Tacitus, *Annals*, XV.xxxx.

In the fire's aftermath, Nero and the Senate were faced with the incredibly daunting job of providing aid to these displaced multitudes. Tacitus recorded Nero's response, which was given in hopes of gaining the favor of the populace: The emperor ordered the opening of "...the Campus Martinus and the public buildings of Agrippa, and his own gardens, and raised temporary structures to receive the destitute multitudes. Supplies of food were brought from Ostia and the neighboring towns and the price of corn was reduced...."[2]

However, as popular as these actions were with the people, Nero's calculated philanthropy was not enough to satiate Rome. In fact, his reputation was worsening at a drastic rate because of the rumor that was circulating through every corner of the city that Nero himself had been responsible for the blaze.

To make matters worse, Nero soon began construction on a massive palace directly in the center of the city in an area cleared by the fire, complete with lush gardens and a 120-foot-tall statue of himself in the courtyard. Although Nero also spearheaded building projects in the wake of the fire that were beneficial to the city, this particular project seemed ostentatious and selfish in the eyes of many and only exacerbated his guilt in the eyes of the people.

With accusations abounding, the emperor felt his grasp on the throne slipping. It seemed inevitable that unless something drastic occurred, he would soon be tried, convicted, and executed for his crimes. Then Nero thought of a diabolical solution to his dilemma. He would place the blame for the fire entirely on the shoulders of an obscure religious sect that had recently come to prominence in Rome — *the Christians*!

Sadly, Nero's scheme was very effective. In the years leading up to the Great Fire, Christians had become unpopular among the people of Rome for a variety of reasons. Therefore, when

---

[2] Tacitus, XV.xxxviiii.

Nero made his public proclamation damning Christians as the chief arsonists, Rome took up the battle cry and attention quickly shifted from him.

Angry and desperate, the people of Rome lashed out against Nero's scapegoat, and Roman authorities began to round up Christians so they could be punished for their supposed crimes. Persecution against followers of Jesus had officially begun in force. This tragic time would leave an indelible mark on the Church and would usher in a period of periodic, intense persecution that would literally span centuries and haunt believers until the eventual collapse of Roman paganism in the Fourth Century.

WHY BLAME CHRISTIANS?

Why would Nero fixate on Christians as a scapegoat for the Great Fire? The reasons for this are complex and multifaceted.

First, to the Roman mind, *Christians were atheists*. This accusation might seem bizarre today, but in order to understand the predicament of the Early Church, one must try to imagine how the Christian faith appeared from the pagan perspective. Christians didn't worship a physical representation of their God, whereas good pagan Romans had all kinds of statues of gods and goddesses on display in their homes to show their religious devotion. And because Christians didn't own or venerate any form of idols, the Romans concluded that they were godless atheists.

Second, *Christians regularly conducted illegal meetings*. According to the law of the Roman Empire in the First Century, it was illegal for any group to hold meetings unless they had the approval of the government. Paranoia was ever-present among Rome's leaders; therefore, they wanted to ensure that dissidents weren't secretly meeting to plot their downfall. If a group desired to hold a meeting, the government wanted to know where that meeting was to be held, who was going to speak, and what the intention of the gathering was. Should a group congregate without seeking this approval, they were deemed to be an illegal gathering and possibly even subverters of the government. Because Nero hated Christians, they were never given official approval to meet. Therefore, each time these early believers met for church, they were *breaking the law* and placing their lives in jeopardy.

Third, *Christians spoke of another King and another Kingdom.* Today we understand that they were referring to the Kingdom of God and the Lordship of Jesus Christ. However, we must remember that Nero had never given believers permission to meet in public where people could have overheard Christian teaching and understood the spiritual nature of this message. Instead, early Christians were forced underground to hold *secret, private meetings*.

Consequently, strange rumors began circulating about the Early Church and its belief. Because believers talked about establishing another Kingdom on earth, Roman leaders interpreted this literally as seeds of rebellion. This was considered treason according to Roman law.

Fourth, *Christians held festivals called "love feasts."* A "love feast" was an event where believers gathered to enjoy a celebratory dinner with other saints and share the love of Jesus. However, to the carnal Roman mind, a "love feast" sounded very much like a pagan orgy. Therefore, Christians were rumored to *be sexual deviants*.

Fifth, *Christians had another ceremonial meeting where they experienced a rite known as "Communion."* Many Romans had heard that the leader of the Christian faith, Jesus of Nazareth, had said, "...Except ye eat the flesh of the Son of man, and drink his blood, ye have no life in you" (John 6:53). On the basis of this statement, it was rumored that Christians gathered privately to practice *cannibalism* — that they were, in fact, eating actual flesh and drinking actual blood. This rumor became so widespread that the Early Church fought accusations of cannibalism for nearly three centuries!

Sixth, *Christians were known to preach about an impending fire that would purge the world.* Since it was common knowledge that Christians spoke of a future great fire, it was easy for Nero to blame them when Rome went up in flames. With this last allegation, Nero drove the final nail into the coffins of countless believers. He convinced the Senate and people of Rome that it was these atheistic subverters of government — *these sexually immoral, cannibalistic, damnation-declarers* — who had started the fire and burned down their beloved city. And although it is certain that not all of Rome believed Nero, he had enough support among the masses that he was able to begin waging a bloody persecution against the Church.

A DARK HOUR FOR THE EARLY CHURCH

In the immediate wake of Nero's proclamation, the situation changed drastically for the Early Church. In the Church's infancy, Christianity had been tolerated by Rome just like any other foreign religion found in the lands of the vast empire. In this environment of relative peace, the Church had grown by leaps and bounds — but suddenly it was no longer being tolerated.

In Rome especially and in other larger cities across the empire, many Christians were hunted down and subjected to rigorous trials, long imprisonments, vicious tortures, and gruesome deaths. The means by which Nero and Roman authorities devised to dispatch their Christian prisoners were unimaginably horrifying and diverse.

Tacitus wrote about these horrors, saying, "...Nero fastened the guilt and inflicted the most exquisite tortures on a class hated for their abominations, called Christians.... Accordingly, an arrest was first made of all who pleaded guilty; then, upon their information, an immense multitude was convicted, not so much of the crime of firing the city, as of hatred against mankind. Mockery of every sort was added to their deaths. Covered with the skins of beasts, they were torn by dogs and perished, or were nailed to crosses, or were doomed to the flames and burnt, to serve as a nightly illumination, when daylight had expired." [3]

The devil was out to destroy Christianity — just as he is in this present day. In the First Century, Satan tried to scare the early believers out of their Christian commitment with the threat of a gruesome death. This type of demonic strategy that the Early Church faced is playing out in certain parts of this war-torn world even today. With every means at his disposal, both subtle and overt, the enemy is trying to instill fear into the hearts of believers. He knows that if he can't get God's people to succumb to a spirit of fear, a torrent of God's power will be released on the earth!

> With every means at his disposal, both subtle and overt, the enemy is trying to instill fear into the hearts of believers. He knows that if he can't get God's people to succumb to a spirit of fear, a torrent of God's power will be released on the earth!

Nero was *determined* to get rid of the Christians, and he endeavored to do this in the most sadistic, evil ways. As Tacitus wrote, Nero even resorted to dousing Christians in wax and then burning them at the stake in his personal garden to serve as lights as he entertained guests! However, as

---

[3] Tacitus, *Annals*, XV.44.

sickening as these acts were, there was also victory to be found in the midst of the tragedy. Early writings hold many stories of pagan onlookers who converted to Christ after observing the joyful, courageous endurance with which many early Christians faced death.

Sadly, not every Christian was so bold when his or her faith was put to the test. Some even defected from the Church — *and this is where the real battle began.* Yes, Nero instigated terrible tribulation. But his persecution was minor in comparison to the compromise that was emerging *inside* the Church — a spiritual infection that would dramatically impact the Body of Christ for centuries to come.

This seems to have been the situation Timothy was dealing with. As persecution increased against the Church during Nero's reign, Timothy was finding that the biggest battle was occurring within the walls of the Church, not in the pagan courts of Rome.

> **This is always what occurs during a fiery trial — *the trial reveals the true depth of people's commitment.***

Paul's second letter to Timothy was written from prison in approximately 67 AD when Nero was at the peak of his madness before he committed suicide a year later. We can surmise from Paul's words in this letter that Timothy was facing issues with *betrayers, defectors,* and *deceivers* within his congregation. This is always what occurs during a fiery trial — *the trial reveals the true depth of people's commitment.*

We Are Called To Stand!

Every pastor has had his or her heart broken, just as Timothy did, by people who abandoned that local congregation. At least in Timothy's day, early believers were leaving largely because they were afraid of being murdered. But if the Lord viewed the desertion of early believers to be a lack of faith, think about how frivolous He would view the excuses of most believers today!

There *are* valid reasons to leave a church. For instance, if doctrinal error is being taught, or if immoral practices are taking place among the leadership or being condoned, it's appropriate to find a new church home. It's also true that believers are at times led of the Lord to move to a new location or to a new local body of believers as part of His plan for their lives.

Nevertheless, in many cases, when people leave their church, it's often an issue of commitment. Spouting off excuses disguised in a cloak of spirituality, uncommitted believers often abandon their spiritual homes in order to avoid responsibility.

Time and trouble always reveal the true commitment of people. Timothy's church was experiencing a defection because of persecution and the imminent threat of death. Yet no matter how difficult the circumstances become, Christians are not called to defect from the place God has ordained them to be planted. *They are called to stand!*

> No matter how difficult the circumstances become, Christians are not called to defect from the place God has ordained them to be planted. *They are called to stand!*

As you study Second Timothy, you will see that this young minister was *overwhelmed* with the onslaught coming against the members of his own church. Some of the believers stood firm, but others were deserting Timothy, deserting their church — and, most importantly, they were deserting *the Lord.*

ADVICE FOR THOSE LIVING
IN THEIR OWN PERSONAL COMBAT ZONE

Hearing about Timothy's struggles, Paul wrote to his young disciple. He began in Second Timothy 1:1,2 by saying, "Paul, an apostle of Jesus Christ by the will of God, according to the promise of life which is in Christ Jesus, To Timothy, my dearly beloved son: grace, mercy, and peace, from God the Father and Christ Jesus our Lord."

By writing these opening lines, Paul deviated from his normal salutation. In most of his epistles, Paul began with the phrase, "Grace and peace be unto you...." However, in Second Timothy 1:2, Paul wrote, "...Grace, *and mercy*, and peace...." This is very important. Paul inserts the word "mercy" into the salutation of his epistles in only three instances: in First Timothy, Second Timothy, and Titus.

In each of these cases, Paul was writing to people who felt *overwhelmed* by their situations. For instance, when Paul penned First Timothy, Timothy had just assumed the leading role in the rapidly growing church of Ephesus, and he felt overwhelmed with his new responsibilities. Because of the awesome task at hand, Timothy needed more than grace and peace; he needed to be reminded that God's *mercy* was available to help him in his situation.

At the time Paul wrote his second epistle to Timothy, the younger minister was struggling because his church members were defecting; his congregation was in decline; and he was overcome with feelings of hurt, rejection, anger, and fear. To continue his work in the Lord, Timothy needed a special measure of God's *mercy*, so Paul reminded him that God's mercy was available to him.

Finally, Paul inserted the words "and mercy" in his greeting to Titus. Imagine what Titus must have felt when Paul left him on the island of Crete to establish a church among the island's unruly inhabitants! A Cretian prophet once had even described his own people by saying, "...The Cretians are always liars, evil beasts, slow bellies...." Paul agreed with this assessment, asserting that "...this witness is true..." (Titus 1:12,13). It would have been very difficult to start a church with people like that! Titus needed to know that a special measure of mercy was available to him for his difficult task. He needed *mercy* to work with the Cretians!

Isn't it good to know that God will do that for you when He calls you to do something difficult? When you are facing a task that overwhelms you, makes you feel inadequate, or seems larger than life itself — He graciously inserts extra mercy between His grace and His peace!

I want you to know that there is a special measure of mercy available to those who feel overwhelmed by trials in life. This was especially good news for young Timothy. But it's good news for you as well because, like Timothy, if you plan to do anything significant for God, you will also find yourself living in a combat zone from time to time!

CHAPTER TWO

OVERCOMING THE SPIRIT OF FEAR

*T*imothy was facing threatening times, so Paul didn't go far in his second letter to the younger minister before he reminded him of a crucial truth: "…God hath not given us the spirit of fear; but of power, and of love, and of a sound mind" (2 Timothy 1:7). This Greek word for "fear" conveys the idea of *cowardice*, and the use of this word identified Timothy's real problem, as we will see.

Fear is a powerful force — and if fear gets a grip on your mind, it will produce cowardice in you. If you let it go unchecked, eventually you'll become afraid of everything and everyone. If you allow it to do so, fear will eventually control your life.

Years ago, I took an informal survey in many churches where I conducted meetings in order to discover what fears people were dealing with in their personal lives. I was shocked to see so much fear, manifested in so many forms, in the Body of Christ. I saw fear of divorce, fear of cancer, fear of AIDS, fear of suicide, fear of insanity, fear of heights, fear of murder, fear of robbers, fear of attack, fear of financial failure, fear of demons, and so on. That was mainly among the laity. Those in the ministry had their own set of fears — fear of rejection, fear of failure, fear of lack of finances, fear of betrayal, fear of being left behind by their peers, and even fear of success!

This makes it clear why we must remember that the Bible says, "For God hath not given us the spirit of fear; but of power, and of love, and of a *sound mind.*"

A SAVED BRAIN AND DELIVERED HEAD!

The words "sound mind" are translated from the Greek word *sophronismos.* This is a compound of the word *sodzo*, which means *salvation* or *deliverance*, and the word *phroneo*, which denotes the *mind* or *intelligence.*

When these two words are compounded, the new word conveys something very important. The word *sophronismos* literally refers to *a mind that is delivered or saved.* I have jokingly called this "*a saved brain*" or "*a delivered head.*" Our minds should not be affected by fear and circumstances, because they have been delivered!

Hebrews 2:15 says that Jesus came to "…deliver them who through fear of death were all their lifetime *subject to bondage.*" This is part of our Christian heritage! Freedom from fear belongs to us. Jesus came to deliver us from fear and to give us a sound mind — *a mind that shouldn't even have to comprehend fear.*

A SPECIAL WORKING OF GOD'S POWER

In Second Timothy 1:8, Paul wrote, "Be not thou therefore ashamed of *the testimony of our Lord*, nor of *me his prisoner*: but be thou partaker of the afflictions of the gospel according to the power of God." According to this verse, Timothy was being tempted to be ashamed of two things — *the testimony of the Lord* and *Paul, the prisoner of the Lord.*

Why do you suppose Timothy was becoming ashamed of the Lord and of Paul, his own father in the faith? To fully understand Timothy's fearful mindset, one must look back at the nature of the turbulent political climate Christians were facing at that time.

In the wake of the great fire of Rome in 64 AD, Nero not only blamed the widespread destruction on the Christians living in the city, but some evidently laid blame on the apostle Paul as one of the instigators for the inferno because he was such a visible Christian leader. Early Christian writers record that Paul was martyred in Rome by Nero's order in the aftermath of the Great Fire.[4] Consequently, being identified with Paul became very dangerous. A personal friend of the apostle would have understood the very real possibility that his name could be added to his list of accomplices!

It is an inescapable fact — verified in Scripture and throughout historical records — that hardships, and often persecutions, come to believers. However, if those believers will stand true to the testimony of the Lord, *there is a special working of God's power available to them.* This is why Paul wrote in verse 8, "...Be thou partaker of the afflictions of the gospel *according to the power of God.*" It was this special working of God's power that operated through brave martyrs in those early centuries of the Church. They would sing praises or quote Scripture as they faced horrific deaths at the hands of their persecutors.

Mentions of these special manifestations of God's power are found throughout Scripture. First Peter 4:14 says, "If ye be reproached for the name of Christ, happy are ye; for the spirit of glory and of God resteth upon you: on their part he is evil spoken of, but on your part he is glorified." God's glory and power always come to rest on those who have entrusted their very lives to Him and are being persecuted or attacked for His sake.

---

[4] Eusebius, *Church History*, III.1.

PAUL'S TESTIMONY

By the time Paul wrote the book of Second Timothy — his very last epistle — he was no longer a young man. In addition, with the exception of Dr. Luke, Paul was all by himself. Luke had faithfully accompanied Paul through every season of his life, but all of Paul's other associates — those people the apostle had regarded as his best friends — began disappearing soon after he was arrested.

However, notice that Paul was *encouraging Timothy*, even though he himself had experienced the biting pain of rejection. Honestly, Timothy was in far better shape than Paul, who had been forsaken on a *massive* scale.

When Paul wrote to Timothy in Second Timothy 1:8, the apostle admonished the younger minister to "...be a partaker of the afflictions of the gospel according to the power of God." Paul *knew* what he was talking about! He had been a partaker of those afflictions on all fronts!

To undergird his encouragement to Timothy, Paul told his own amazing story of the hard knocks he had weathered in life. It's almost as if Paul wanted Timothy to know that he, too, had been through difficult times and thus he had a right to say, *"Hang in there."*

Paul began his testimony in Second Timothy 1:15 by saying, "This thou knowest, that all they which are in Asia be turned away from me...."

Can you imagine what it would be like to have an entire geographical region of people reject you? That is exactly what Paul experienced. He explicitly stated, "...*All* they which are in Asia be turned away from me...." Think about that. Paul could have written the book on rejection! He had an entire region of believers — *throughout the province of Asia* — turn away from him!

Paul continued his testimony in verses 16 and 17 by saying, "The Lord give mercy unto the household of Onesiphorus; for he oft refreshed me, and was not ashamed of my chain: But, when he was in Rome, he sought me out very diligently, and found me."

In essence Paul was saying, *"I do have at least one man who has remained faithful to me. Thank God for Onesiphorus."*

Paul understood rejection. He had been forsaken by some of his closest friends and, even more, by all the churches in Asia. The province of Asia is where the apostle had accomplished some of his most significant work for the Lord. As such, this must have been an especially difficult rejection for Paul to bear. Like it or not, some people do go AWOL in the midst of spiritual warfare. Paul must have been shocked to discover that many of his own friends had become guilty of such desertion.

'FOUGHT IT, FINISHED IT, KEPT IT' — STRONG WARRIORS STAND STRONG!

However, despite the great difficulties Paul faced, he still maintained a victorious attitude. He didn't allow these rejections to drag him down. He didn't get angry and resentful at anyone, and he refused to hold a grudge.

In Second Timothy 4:6 and 7, Paul wrote, "For I am now ready to be offered, and the time of my departure is at hand. I have fought a good fight, I have finished my course, I have kept the faith."

Paul was even facing death, yet he was victorious! When he wrote, "I have fought a good fight...," the word "fight" is the

Greek word *agonidzo*, which is where we get the word *agony*. By using this word, Paul was telling us that some of his ministry had been *pure agony — an unbelievably difficult contest* that we will study in detail further on in this chapter. However, Paul had not budged an inch. He stayed in the fight and remained faithful to his call!

In this verse, the Greek sentence structure is actually reversed. It should say, "*A GOOD FIGHT — I fought one!*" The emphasis is on *the fight*. These were the sentiments of a man who had no regrets. Paul was proud of the contest he had been in. Regardless of all the others who dropped out of the fight, he could say, "*I stayed in there. A GOOD FIGHT — fought it!*"

Then Paul continued, saying, "…I have finished my course…." This word "course" is actually the Greek word *dromos*, which always describes *a foot race* or *a running track*. Notice how Paul personalized this by saying "my course." He didn't attempt to run anyone else's course. He stayed right on track — true to God's call on his life. Although many others had fallen out of their race and cancelled their fight, Paul could victoriously state, "*Not me! I didn't fall out! I finished my assignment!*" Again, the Greek structure is reversed. A better translation would be: "*MY RACE — I finished it!*"

> Paul was proud of the contest he had been in. Regardless of all the others who dropped out of the fight, he could say, "I stayed in there. *A GOOD FIGHT — I fought it!*"

Next, Paul proclaimed, "…I have kept the faith." The Greek word for "kept" is the word *tereo*, which conveys the idea of *remaining true to a commitment*. This shows that, spiritually, Paul was far ahead of the rest of the gang who were *not* keeping the faith. They were actually letting go of their faith in order to save their skin! But Paul could say, *"Not me! I kept the faith!"* Like Paul's preceding statements, the Greek actually reverses the structure of this phrase as well. It reads, *"THE FAITH — I kept it!"*

This soldier of the Lord had *everything* to shout about! Paul's ministry may have been difficult — one that was lived out in the combat zone — but *he didn't relinquish an inch to the enemy*! And as Paul faced his own death, he knew he had done well. He declared, *"A GOOD FIGHT, I really fought myself one!"*

Instead of fearing death, Paul was excited to depart and meet the Lord. In Second Timothy 4:8, he said, "Henceforth there is laid up for me a crown of righteousness, which the Lord, the righteous judge, shall give me at that day: and not to me only, but unto all them also that love his appearing."

Notice what he said: "…which the Lord, the righteous judge, shall give me *at that day*…." *Paul knew his day of departure was imminent.*

Remember, in verse 6 Paul had written, "For I am now ready *to be offered*, and the time of *my departure* is at hand." He could have been thinking about how they were going to kill him. He might have wondered what the blade would feel like if it hit the back of his neck. *Would he feel it? Would it hurt?*

But instead of giving place to those fearful thoughts, Paul talked about "departing" — not about *dying*. He was ready to go. He was a soldier who, at the end of his life, was proud of the fight he had fought, the race he had run, and the faith he had kept. *Paul had absolutely no regrets!*

PAUL'S OWN COMBAT-ZONE STORY

In Second Timothy 4:9-11, Paul continued relating his testimony to Timothy. Remember, Paul wasn't telling his story in order to make Timothy feel sorry for him; rather, he was building a foundation from which to speak to Timothy. When Paul told Timothy to be strong in the midst of battle, he knew what he was talking about! He had been in the midst of battle himself.

With this in mind, let's continue reading Paul's testimony of the hard knocks he endured — *a story from his own combat zone.*

Paul wrote in Second Timothy 4:9-11, "Do thy diligence to come shortly unto me: For Demas hath forsaken me, having loved this present world, and is departed unto Thessalonica; Crescens to Galatia, Titus unto Dalmatia. Only Luke is with me...."

Who was Demas? Demas was noted among the apostles, and he is spoken highly of in Scripture. For instance, in Colossians 4, Paul mentioned Demas alongside:

- Onesimus (v. 9), who is called "a faithful and beloved brother."

- Aristarchus (v. 10), who is called a "fellow-prisoner."

- Mark (v. 10), whom the saints were instructed to "receive."

- Justus (v. 11), whom Paul called "my fellow-worker" and a "comfort."

- Epaphras (v. 12), who always labored fervently in prayer (v. 13).

- The saints, for whom he had "great zeal" (v. 13).

Finally, in verse 14, Demas is mentioned in the very same sentence as Luke. Verse 14 states, "Luke, the beloved physician, and Demas, greet you."

Demas had been an important leader in the Early Church. This is an important fact because it reveals that fear can affect any Christian if he or she allows it — regardless of his or her status in the Church. Even with his many years of ministry behind him and a slew of powerful Christian associates to lean on, Demas gave way to fear and "departed" when the situation became too tough! As Paul related the story to Timothy, it's almost as if he said, *"You're not going to believe this one — even Demas has left me!"*

In addition, as Paul related in verse 10, his associates Crescens and Titus had also gone to take up ministry elsewhere. All things considered, Paul was left in a very isolated position, with only Luke remaining at his side.

The Sustained Fortitude of Luke

Paul's relationship with Luke was a long-lasting one. It's a historical fact that everywhere Paul went, Luke went too. This is the reason Luke could write the book of Acts with such accuracy — he knew everything Paul did because he traveled to most places with him. Luke even willingly went to prison for periods of time so he could be close to Paul! *What a beautiful picture of covenant relationship this is!*

Why did Luke stick so close to Paul's side? For one thing, Paul was repeatedly beaten and tortured, so it's very likely that Luke accompanied the apostle to provide him with medical treatment if he needed care.

As Christians, we believe in divine healing, and we *know* that the Bible promises it. But consider your course of action if you hurt yourself badly in some way, such as running into a barbed wire fence and gouging your arm. Of course, you'd pray for your arm to be healed. But if your arm wasn't quickly healed, you'd naturally say to yourself, *I have to do something to alleviate this pain and stop the bleeding.*

Paul had been repeatedly beaten and tortured on numerous occasions. We know he had supernatural power flowing through him to heal his body; otherwise, his body couldn't have kept going. It literally would have been impossible. The persecutions he suffered were that severe!

This is why Paul could write in Romans 8:11, "But if the Spirit of him that raised up Jesus from the dead dwell in you, he that raised up Christ from the dead shall also quicken your mortal bodies by his Spirit that dwelleth in you." Paul knew firsthand of the Holy Spirit's quickening power!

THE INTENSE PERSECUTIONS PAUL SUFFERED

To get a better sense of the persecutions Paul endured, let's look at Second Corinthians 11:24,25. It says, "Of the Jews five times received I forty stripes save one. Thrice was I beaten with rods, once was I stoned, thrice I suffered shipwreck, a night and a day I have been in the deep."

Let's examine these persecutions one by one. Paul began verse 24 by mentioning a severe punishment he had received from the Jews: "Of the Jews five times received I forty stripes save one...."

This was not a beating with a bullwhip as most might suppose. *This was a brutal ordeal undertaken with a special weapon of torture intended to teach its victim an unforgettable lesson.*

The victim had his clothes removed, and he was tied to a post, unable to move a hand to defend himself. The whip used in such beatings was often constructed of three long, separate straps of animal hide, bound together at the base and then tied to a very long handle. At times, pieces of bone and glass were even attached to the ends of these straps in order to inflict more pain and suffering upon the victim.

Rather than simply striking the victim, those carrying out the punishment were taught to hit hard and wrap the multiple straps of hide around the victim's body. Then instead of letting the straps fall naturally to the ground, the weapon was quickly jerked while the straps were still around the body, which would cause skin to be ripped off, leaving horrible, gaping wounds.

If the straps had bone and glass attached to their ends, the bone and glass would lodge in the skin, and when the straps were jerked back, those pieces of bone and glass would *tear out* pieces of flesh. One-third of the stripes were given across the upper chest and face, and the last two-thirds were given across the back while the victim remained in a bent-over position.

Receiving these stripes at the hands of Jewish authorities was truly an awful, brutal, bloody, excruciating ordeal.

DID PAUL WALK IN FAITH?

Paul stated, "...Five times received I forty stripes save one" (2 Corinthians 11:24). Therefore, he had endured this grueling experience on five different occasions — with one-third on the front of his upper chest and face, and the rest on his lower back and legs.

The very fact that Paul *could* go through these ordeals and still walk and function to continue his ministry is profound evidence that he *did* walk in faith. Paul *never* gave in. The devil could not stop this soldier from fighting! It was his faith that carried him through every ordeal to victory.

In verse 25, Paul immediately mentioned the next type of persecution he had experienced. He wrote, "Thrice was I beaten with rods...."

In the ancient world, being beaten with rods was a horrible form of torture that was regularly used. Contrary to common belief, this was not simply the act of hitting a victim with a stick. In fact, it was far worse than this!

Beating with rods was inflicted by Roman civil authorities and usually executed by *lictors*, or especially appointed bodyguards of the principal magistrate who were responsible for enforcing his legal judgments. Standing authoritatively at the side of their governor, lictors wielded a symbolic weapon known as the *facses*, which was essentially a bundle of birch rods bound around an axe.[5] Some scholars believe that the bundle of rods was actually used by the lictor to carry out punishment, especially during the Imperial Period — the centuries when emperors ruled the Roman Empire (27 BC to approximately 476 AD). The punishment would be carried out by binding the prisoner's arms tightly around his body, similar to the way a straitjacket binds a person's arms. Then the lictor would use the rods to inflict severe beatings on the prisoner's body, including even the bottoms of his feet.

> Paul *never* gave in. The devil could not stop this soldier from fighting! It was his faith that carried him through every ordeal to victory.

Once again, the severity of this punishment shows that God's power was available and was working in Paul. The fact that this punishment was inflicted upon him three separate times reveals that Paul was supernaturally strengthened and restored after each event.

As if being whipped and beaten wasn't enough, Paul went on to mention his next memory of persecution, saying, "...Once was I stoned..." (v. 25).

---

[5] Smith, Sir William; Cornish, F. Warre, ed., *A Concise Dictionary of Greek and Roman Antiquities* London: John Murray), p. 387.

Stoning was another vicious type of torture. The victim was normally placed in the bottom of a pit or at the foot of a hill with his hands and legs bound tightly. Standing around the rim of a pit, a crowd would gather above with large stones (*not* pebbles!). Then they would all simultaneously begin hurling their stones down upon the unfortunate victim, specifically aiming for the head. In fact, they would often hurl stones until the victim's head was completely crushed, ensuring his death.

Paul's testimony of being stoned in Second Corinthians 11:25 is generally believed to be the same stoning recorded in Acts 14:19. It reads, "And there came thither certain Jews from Antioch and Iconium, who persuaded the people, and, having stoned Paul, drew him out of the city, supposing he had been dead."

Paul's experience here was deadly. Someone may say, "Doesn't the fact that this happened to Paul show a lack of faith on his part?" *Absolutely not!* In fact, it reveals Paul that had incredible faith — because he didn't stop preaching the Gospel in obedience to God, nor did he *stay* dead! Acts 14:20 says, "Howbeit, as the disciples stood round about him, *he rose up....*" From Paul's own testimony in Second Corinthians 11 and 12, we know that he had died and been resurrected at least once in his ministry. This shows *tremendous* faith!

In Second Corinthians 11:25 and 26, Paul finished relating his testimony, writing, "... I suffered shipwreck, a night and a day have I been in the deep; in journeyings often, in perils of waters, in perils of robbers, in perils by mine own countrymen, in perils by the heathen, in perils in the city, in perils in the wilderness, in perils in the sea, in perils among false brethren." Paul's list of hardships was *extreme* and *extensive*.

WHEN THE LORD STANDS BY YOU

Thus, to say that Paul needed Dr. Luke's help from time to time doesn't negate the healing power of God. The Holy Spirit had quickened Paul's body on many occasions. But if Paul needed medical attention as that healing power was being manifested, Luke was at his side, committed to helping the apostle recover.

In addition to Luke, we learn in Second Timothy 4:19-21 that four other believers in Rome also remained true to their relationship with Paul. He mentioned them, saying, "Do thy diligence to come before winter. Eubulus greeteth thee, and Pudens, and Linus, and Claudia, and all the brethren." The phrase "all the brethren" refers to the church in Rome. These believers, which were mentioned by name — Eubulus, Pudens, Linus, and Claudia — were not afraid to be closely associated with Paul, and the apostle was very grateful for their loyalty.

Back in Second Timothy 4:16, Paul went on to describe another tragic moment of betrayal in his life. He says, "At my first answer no man stood with me, but all men forsook me: I pray God that it may not be laid to their charge."

The word "stood" is the Greek word *paregeneto*, a term used to describe *a witness who stands forward in a court of law to support a prisoner.* By selecting this word, Paul made his point clear. When he desperately needed the support of his fellow believers, they weren't willing to be associated with him. He had been betrayed. No one stood forward to support him.

In fact, Paul went on to say, "...But all men forsook me...." The word "forsook" means *to leave in the lurch* or *to leave at the worst possible moment.* It conveys the idea of *abandonment.* Paul was painting a clear picture. He was saying, in essence, "*Not only did they not come forward to support me and stand with me — but they also left me at the worst possible moment. They couldn't have picked a worse moment to do what they did."*

You'd think these horror stories would have made Paul bitter, but there was absolutely no bitterness in him. The apostle had learned a marvelous secret: *If no one else will stand with you, the Lord will be faithful to come forward to stand alongside you, support you, and help you.*

Continuing in verse 17, Paul said, "Notwithstanding the Lord stood with me, and strengthened me; that by me the preaching might be fully known, and that all the Gentiles might hear: and I was delivered out of the mouth of the lion."

Look at what the Lord did for this apostle! First, Paul said, "…The Lord *stood* with me…." This word "stood" in Greek is *paristemi*, which means *to stand by one's side.* By using this word, Paul told us Jesus Christ is not ashamed of any faithful soldier. *If no one else will come to your aid, Jesus Christ will come to your rescue.*

Second, Paul wrote that Jesus "strengthened" him. That word "strengthened" in Greek is the word *endunameo*, which always refers to *an empowerment* or *inner strengthening.* It's where we get the word "endued." This was the very word Paul used in Second Timothy 2:1 when he told Timothy to "…be strong in the grace that is in Christ Jesus."

> **If no one else will stand with you, the Lord will be faithful to come forward to stand alongside you, support you, and help you.**

What was the result of this situation? Paul revealed the outcome, saying, "…I was delivered out of the mouth of the lion" (2 Timothy 4:17).

Divine Aid To Sustain Intense Pressure

Let's look for a moment at the example of Jesus. In His final hours in Gethsemane, Jesus was nearly overwhelmed with His own feelings of weakness. In this moment of need, Jesus requested that Peter, James, and John come aside with Him to pray.

Rarely did Jesus need assistance from His disciples — *yet they always needed His*. But in this intense moment, Jesus asked them to pray with Him for just one hour.

Twice Jesus went back to speak with them. But instead of praying, they were sleeping — at the very moment when He desperately needed them!

Have you ever wondered where all of your friends were when you needed them so badly? Jesus Himself was confronted with this same problem.

Often it isn't that people don't care. They simply don't realize the greatness or the heaviness of your burden. It's *your* burden, not theirs; therefore, they may not understand the seriousness of what you're feeling. Of course, you may encounter some people who really *don't* care. But in most cases, you'll find that your friends just aren't fully aware of how great and heavy your burden is.

This was true for Jesus. It was the first time He really needed His disciples to pray with Him, but they kept falling asleep. Jesus had to pray through His heavy burden alone in the Garden of Gethsemane.

In Luke 22:44, the Bible describes the mental and spiritual battle Jesus was experiencing: "And being in an agony he prayed more earnestly: and his sweat was as it were great drops of blood falling down to the ground."

Notice the word "agony." This is from the Greek word *agonidzo*, which always refers *to the most strenuous type of activity*. In this case, the strenuous activity involved all of Jesus' spirit, soul, and body. He was in *agony*.

So intense was this "agony" that the verse continues: "...He prayed more *earnestly*...." "Earnestly" is the Greek word *ektenes*, which describes the condition of a person *stretched and pushed to the limit*. This is the description of a person who is *on the edge*, or *on the brink*, of all that he can possibly endure.

The pressure Jesus felt was so intense that it actually produced a medical condition in His physical body. Verse 44 says, "...And his sweat was as it were *great drops of blood* falling down to the ground." The phrase "great drops of blood" in Greek is the word *thrombos*, which refers to *thick clots of blood*.

A study done by a leading medical school asserts that Jesus experienced a medical condition called *hematidrosis*. This condition exists in those who are in a highly emotional state. The mind is placed under such heavy pressure and stress that it begins to send signals of pressure and stress throughout the body. So strong are these signals that the body begins to respond as if it were under real physical pressure. The second layer of skin separates from the first, forming a vacuum. Blood quickly fills that vacuum and then begins oozing out of the pores of the skin.

This tells us that intense spiritual warfare carries over into mental warfare, which literally affects the physical part of man. This was undoubtedly the worst spiritual combat Jesus had ever been through in His humanity up to this time. And where were His disciples? *They were sleeping!*

But here is the good news! Look at what it says in verse 43: "And there appeared an angel unto him from heaven, strengthening him." When Jesus could find no one to stand with Him in

His hour of need and intense warfare, God provided Him with the help He needed! God sent an angel from Heaven to Jesus in order to strengthen Him.

Regardless of your situation, your battle, or your particular combat zone, God will come to your assistance. If no one else is faithful, He will always remain faithful!

Paul understood this from firsthand experience. Sitting in his prison cell, the apostle found himself abandoned in his time of need. But just as God had provided for Jesus, He provided for Paul.

Therefore, Paul continued in Second Timothy 4:17 by saying, "Notwithstanding the Lord stood with me, and strengthened me...." So great was the impact of God's intervention in Paul's life that the apostle concluded, "And the Lord shall deliver me from every evil work, and will preserve me unto his heavenly kingdom: to whom be glory for ever and ever. Amen" (v. 18).

You say, "Rick, why did you go through this whole scenario?" Because I want you to see that *the apostle Paul was a man who had a platform from which to speak.*

Paul was speaking about the experiences in his own life. He *knew* what it meant to serve God on the front lines of battle. He *knew* what it was like to pour life into someone and then be rejected and forsaken by that person. Paul understood life in the combat zone. *He had a right to speak!* His preaching and teaching were not merely words or the conveying of information. Paul could speak with real authority because he *believed* what he was saying, and he *lived it.*

That's why the words the apostle wrote to the younger minister resonate with the force of seasoned experience when he said, "Thou therefore, my son, *be strong* in the grace that is in Christ

Jesus" (2 Timothy 2:1). And those are words we can take as *our* instruction when we find ourselves in our own personal combat zone. While pursuing what God has asked us to do, we also can be endued with this supernatural grace, strength, and power.

CHAPTER THREE

SUPERNATURAL POWER TO FIGHT AND FORGIVE

*P*aul had lived much of his life in the combat zone, suffering sabotage, rejection, defection, and betrayal. Yet even after all that, the apostle still maintained a victorious attitude that was completely untainted by bitterness. As he faced death, Paul was excited about his remaining days on earth and absolutely thrilled at the prospect of seeing Jesus! In the midst of it all, he had maintained his victory.

You may be asking, "How did Paul do it?" Second Timothy 2:1 reveals the apostle's secret. In this verse, he admonished Timothy, "Thou therefore, my son, be strong in the grace that is in Christ Jesus."

As we saw in the last chapter, this word "strong" is the Greek word *endunameo*, and it refers to *an inner strengthening*. It can also be translated *be empowered*, which refers specifically to a *supernatural empowerment*. So we see that the word "strong," or *endunameo*, refers to a *supernatural touch from God on a person's life that strengthens and empowers*.

> As he faced death, Paul was excited about his remaining days on earth and absolutely thrilled at the prospect of seeing Jesus! In the midst of it all, he had maintained his victory.

Moving Beyond Fear

In Paul's second epistle to Timothy, the apostle addressed his son in the faith about the serious trials Timothy was encountering. He began by calling Timothy to remembrance concerning his spiritual upbringing, his faith, and his holy calling and assignment (*see* 2 Timothy 1:5,6). Then in verse 7, Paul went on to tell Timothy, "For God hath not given us the spirit of fear; but of power, and of love, and of a sound mind."

But in order for Timothy to move *beyond* his fear, he would require a supernatural touch from God. Just telling him to change wouldn't be enough in this case. Timothy was so affected by fear that only a supernatural touch would put him back on his feet again.

By using the Greek word *endunameo*, Paul reminded Timothy that supernatural power was available to assist him during his crisis. Timothy didn't have to face his terrible circumstances alone, and neither do you. God's power was available to give Timothy just what he needed — an inner strengthening and empowering. If Timothy would just reach out and take it by the hand of faith, that divine power was available to him. *And the good news is that it's available to you too!*

There Timothy was — the pastor of a declining, persecuted church. As Timothy had observed the deteriorating situation in the world around him, he apparently had allowed fear to grip him. This fear was so intense that in Second Timothy 1:8, Paul implied that Timothy may have even been thinking about deserting the Lord:

> **Be not thou therefore ashamed of the testimony of our Lord, nor of me his prisoner: but be thou partaker of the afflictions of the gospel according to the power of God.**

It was very significant that this young preacher might think about renouncing the Christian life after all he had seen and learned. Tremendous fear and pain must have gripped his soul. It's evident from Paul's words that the combat zone had almost "fatally wounded" Timothy, and he was thinking about giving up.

With all Timothy's knowledge, experience, and years in the ministry, he was living far below God's plan for his life. This must have produced an incredible sense of failure in him. This great pastoral example was crashing — *right in front of everyone.* If anyone ever needed a fresh supernatural touch of strengthening power, it was Timothy.

This is why Paul said in Second Timothy 2:1, "Thou therefore, my son, be strong *in the grace* that is in Christ Jesus."

This phrase "in the grace" is very important. It carries the idea, *"Be strong by means of the grace that is in Christ Jesus."* God's grace makes this strength available to *every* Christian soldier!

This is great news! God's grace *never* runs out! That means there is a never-ending supply of inner strengthening available to you. All you have to do is reach out and take that supernatural empowering by faith.

You may say, "Well, this *endunameo* is exactly what I need in my life. I'm going through a horrible situation. I'm overwhelmed by all that has come against me from every side! I feel *terrified.* A spirit of fear is trying to wrap itself around me. You're right — I'm paralyzed with fear! *I need a supernatural touch from God."*

If you're going to experience this kind of empowering inner strength, you must receive it *freely* by means of God's grace. You can't walk in this power any other way — by worrying, fretting, trying harder, etc. It's *always* delivered to the saints "by means of grace." So we could translate this verse like this: *"Thou therefore, my son, lay hold of a steady current of God's power, which comes to you as a result of His grace."*

You will find that a steady current of God's power is available to operate in you as long as you're laying hold of His grace. God knows that you need His power to fight in the combat zone, so He makes His grace available to you as you draw near to Him to lay hold of it *by faith* (*see* Ephesus 2:8). This all results from a relationship of *trust* in Him based on His Word and your determination to stay the course and act on what He has said.

IF 'PLAN A' FAILS, WHAT ABOUT 'PLAN B'?

Notice when Timothy was in trouble, Paul *didn't* say, "Thou therefore, my son, *go to Plan B*." Paul also didn't say, "Thou therefore, my son, *resign your church in Ephesus and put out your resume for another pastorate*."

> You will find that a steady current of God's power is available to operate in you as long as you're laying hold of His grace.

What did Paul say instead? He admonished Timothy, *"Stay right there in the midst of your conflict, and grab hold of God's power that is freely made available to you!"*

You must face this fact: If God has called you to do something — no matter what the assignment is — there will be times when hell's forces come against you. At such times, you may be tempted to say, "All right, I've had enough! God, You're going to have to get someone else to do this job, because I've had all I'm going to take!"

So get ready to experience a few tough moments when you want to desert the original plan that God gave you because it seems so difficult to fulfill. In that moment, you may want to pursue Plan B — or even Plan *E*! But settle it within yourself right now — you will *always* encounter some form of opposition as you serve the Lord. If it isn't people who are hurting you, it may be a lack of money that tries to slow you down. If it isn't a lack of money, it may be a shortage of people who will come alongside you and help you fulfill your God-given assignment. If it isn't a shortage of help, it may be a lack of communication in your relationships. If it isn't a lack of communication, it may be a battle with an overwhelming sense of futility and fruitlessness.

We *all* have opportunities and temptations to bail out — sometimes on a daily basis! Therefore, it's vital that we learn how to open our hearts to God and allow Him to give us strength.

God's supernatural strength will empower us to *stay* in the fight, to *keep running* the race, and to *hold on* to the call He first gave us. We must lay hold of a steady current of God's power, which comes to us as a result of His grace!

Regardless of the specifics of your struggle or the depth of your present feelings of failure, you have only two options available to you — either *resign spiritually and give up* or *lay hold of a steady current of God's power*. So what are you going to do? Instead of wallowing in defeat, why don't you reach out and take hold of God's supernatural, transforming power? *It belongs to you!*

> We *all* have opportunities and temptations to bail out — sometimes on a daily basis! Therefore, it's vital that we learn how to open our hearts to God and allow Him to give us strength.

GETTING CLOSE TO OTHER COMBAT-ZONE FIGHTERS

In Second Timothy 2:2, Paul continued his message to Timothy, saying, "And the things that thou hast heard of me among many witnesses, the same commit thou to faithful men, who shall be able to teach others also."

I want you to especially notice the phrase, "And the things that thou hast heard of me...." The word "of" in Greek is the word *para*, which literally means *along* or *alongside*. However, it conveys much more than this. It carries the idea of *partnership*, *a side-by-side relationship*, or *a very close relationship*.

In Second Timothy 2:2, Paul used this word *para* to describe his relationship with Timothy in the past and present. Remember, Timothy and Paul had a longstanding, godly relationship. Timothy was not just someone who sat in the crowd and listened to Paul's sermons. He had traveled with Paul. He had preached with Paul. Timothy had experienced life and ministry *personally* and *up close* with Paul.

By using this word *para*, Paul confirmed his close relationship with Timothy. Verse 2 could be understood as, "The things that thou hast learned *by virtue of our close, longstanding relationship...*"; "the things that thou hast learned *as a result of our side-by-side relationship...*"; or, "the things that thou hast learned *because I allowed you to become so close to me personally....*" These convey the right idea of the word *para*.

This close relationship was the reason Paul could say, "But thou hast *fully known* my doctrine, manner of life, purpose, faith, longsuffering, charity, patience" (2 Timothy 3:10). Timothy was close enough to the apostle to have seen all these qualities that Paul demonstrated in his walk with God.

Paul continued in Second Timothy 2:2, saying, "And the things that thou hast learned of me [*"right next to me, by my side, by virtue of our close, intimate relationship"*], the same commit thou to faithful men, who shall be able to teach others also."

Take note of the phrase "the same," because it's very important. Paul made his message to Timothy very clear after reminding the younger minister of their close relationship. In essence, Paul said, *"Timothy, you know what I have done for you. Now you get back out there and do the same for others."*

Paul's instruction must have seemed like an intimidating prospect for the younger minister. Timothy had selected people for leadership positions before, and it seems that much of his congregation had forsaken him. He had given his life to a group of people once already, and the full context of the passage indicates that Timothy felt many had stabbed him in the back.

When a person has been betrayed or abandoned by others in the past, it can be terrifying to think about becoming vulnerable and putting one's trust in people again. For Timothy, this meant he had to get close to a *new* circle of leaders, allowing them to come alongside him in ministry, walking and talking with them, sharing his life and his heart with them, and fellowshipping with them in a variety of settings. Paul's instruction carried God's challenge to Timothy to lay hold of His grace and receive the supply of divine power needed to forge ahead. Timothy needed to find his new God-assigned team with whom he could come alongside and mentor the way Paul had mentored him.

COMMIT YOURSELF TO SOMEONE!

Paul wasted no time in adding to his command as he addressed Timothy in Second Timothy 2:2. Notice the next word he used:

"...the same *commit thou....*" This word "commit" is also very important because it reveals what Timothy was supposed to do when his new leaders came alongside him.

The word "commit" is the Greek compound word *paratithimi*. *Para* is again the Greek word that speaks of *close relationship*. The second part of the word, *tithimi*, means *to place, to lay*, or *to position something*. When the two words are compounded, the new word describes *the act of depositing something*, such as depositing money or valuables into a place of safekeeping.

You may ask, "How does all this apply to *me?*"

We've all been burned badly at least once in life. If we allow the fear of being hurt again to take root in our hearts, it could cause us to step backward into isolation, never again to develop close relationships and receive a supply from others or to make deposits into others' lives.

If you allow this to occur in your life, you will become "fatally wounded." *Satan's plan will have worked!* It simply isn't possible for you to live and fight in the spiritual combat zone — and *win* — without the assistance of others.

You may have been hurt or betrayed by a brother or sister in Christ — perhaps even by a close friend or a leading member of your local church. The mess you weathered may have just about destroyed you. But what else can you do but forgive those who hurt you, extend grace to them, and start all over again? Any other option will simply lead you into spiritual isolation and defeat.

You really have no other choice but to be open to trust again after being burned by people in the past. I can tell you from hard experience that this isn't always easy. But that doesn't change the fact that it's the only option God gives you.

If you've been wounded in the combat zone, it's time to be restored and healed. Rather than allowing the wound to fester and get worse, you must trust God and open your heart again to pursue the relationships He wants to place in your life. *There is no other choice in Him.*

THE BEST FIGHTERS: 'FAITHFUL MEN'

The number-one reason we get hurt in relationships is not that we let people get close to us; it's that we let the *wrong* people come alongside us in life.

We must learn to be careful about *who* gets close to us. Although we shouldn't judge people or be suspicious about them, it's essential that we stay sensitive to the Holy Spirit's leading and let Him bring people alongside us whom we can trust and relate to. We need people with enough spiritual maturity to understand that we are normal people with imperfections. *And* we need Spirit-filled, character-rich combat fighters standing by our side!

> If you've been wounded in the combat zone, it's time to be restored and healed. Rather than allowing the wound to fester and get worse, you must trust God and open your heart again to pursue the relationships He wants to place in your life. There is no other choice in Him.

Essentially Paul was saying, *"Timothy, the problem is not people. The problem is that you got close to the wrong group of people!"*

Of course, God-called men and women can start out great and then falter later in the race because they failed to lay hold of the grace of God. But there are times when people come alongside you *who should not be there* — who were not called to walk with you in the first place.

Whom you allow next to your side is very important. Remember, you're placing a precious deposit from your own life into them. You don't want to make a foolish mistake that may eventually wound you and hinder you from moving forward in God's plan for your own life. The battle you're fighting is fierce enough — don't provide more ammunition to the opposing forces! Seek the Lord about the people He has called to come alongside you in this season of your life. Make certain you have *His* mind regarding the people to whom He wants you to entrust yourself!

> **Whom you allow next to your side is very important. Remember, you're placing a precious deposit from your own life into them.**

So who *were* the people Timothy needed to consider in selecting his next group of elders and deacons? *Those who had stayed when everyone else left.* These were very possibly the people who should have been Timothy's choices for leadership in the first place!

Those who stayed in Timothy's church were probably not as influential as the others who had left. Most likely all he had left in his congregation were "regular" people — the Early Church equivalent of our modern-day janitors, garbage collectors, greeters, ushers, "support" ministry, and so on. But when everyone else left, these people stayed true. They probably fit into the category the Bible talks about — those humble before the Lord who were there because they served Christ (*see* Colossians 3:24), not because of title, influence, recognition, or even money.

Don't you thank God for all your friends who have remained true to you through the years? Early in your life, you may think friends come a dime a dozen. But as life goes on and you mature, you realize that your list of genuine friends gets smaller and smaller.

There are several reasons for this. Life gets busy; people move from one city to another; jobs change; people switch churches, and so on. The friendships that endure it all are *precious gifts*. Thank God for a real friend who is faithful through it all!

This is why Paul wrote, "And the things that thou hast heard of me...the same commit thou to *faithful* men, who shall be able to teach others also" (2 Timothy 2:2).

Timothy understood Paul's message. He knew that Paul meant, *"The things you heard from me while you were next to my side, get out there and do for others! You must affix your life to a new group of people. However, make sure you entrust yourself to FAITH-FUL men!"*

Notice that Paul emphasized faithfulness and *not* ability. He didn't say, "Commit thou to *qualified* men." That's another thing I've learned from hard experience — that there are many qualified people whom a leader does *not* want doing the job! That's why Paul said, "Commit thou to *faithful* men."

Certainly it's good if you can find a qualified person to fill a certain position, but Paul says the first priority is to look for "*faithful* men." If you can find a faithful person who is also qualified, you've come across a real jewel! Faithfulness, however, is what you should seek first.

> If you can find a faithful person who is also qualified, you've come across a real jewel! Faithfulness, however, is what you should seek first.

For example, there are many people who can handle money wisely, but they aren't necessarily the right people to put in charge of the church treasury. They may step into that position and just try to take over! They may want to control every penny and correct the leadership every time those God has placed in charge want to do something

If you are a church leader and you choose someone too hastily for a position, you may very well end up praying that person out of the position — while hoping it can be done without causing a church rift.

And when it comes to choosing the right people for your advisory board, make sure you have the mind of God on the matter. You want people who won't allow that position of trust and responsibility to go to their heads. Otherwise, you may have board members who want to tell you what to preach and what not to preach. *Look for faithfulness!*

> **How we treat others is a mark of our maturity or *lack* of maturity.**

As believers, we are brothers and sisters who will spend eternity together, regardless of how we treat each other here on earth. God cares more than we've realized about how we treat others, and He uses our attitudes toward and our treatment of others as a measuring rod for promotion. How we treat others is a mark of our maturity or *lack* of maturity.

But not everyone lives with eternity in view or conducts their lives conscious and aware of God's divine presence. That's why we must make wise choices in the selection of our *close* friends and associates. Otherwise, we open ourselves up to hurts and wounds that can infect our hearts and remove us temporarily — and sometimes even *permanently* — from our personal fight of faith to fulfill God's call on our lives.

A Proper Heart Attitude

Qualification is not enough! *Faithfulness is the real issue.* That is why Paul wrote, "...Commit thou to *faithful men,* who shall *be able....*"

The word "able" in this verse is extremely important to the subject at hand. In Greek, it's the word *hikanos,* which conveys the idea of *sufficiency.* Notice how Paul began to describe the faithful men: "...who shall *be able....*" A better translation would be "...who shall *be sufficient....*"

Paul was teaching that "faithful men" may not be qualified for the task *right now,* but because of their proper heart attitude, they can become *sufficient* for the task. You see, God doesn't call people because of their talent. He doesn't call people because He is impressed with their qualifications. *God calls people because their hearts are right.*

I once met a man who wanted to be used of the Lord. I asked him what he was waiting on. He replied, "Well, I'm a garbage collector." He was embarrassed by his occupation, and he thought no garbage collector could ever go into the ministry.

Do you know why he thought this? Because being a garbage collector is a dirty job. It's not like being a bank president or a physician. He was embarrassed about his job and didn't think he could ever be used of the Lord in full-time service.

> God doesn't call people because of their talent. He doesn't call people because He is impressed with their qualifications. *God calls people because their hearts are right.*

However, most calls to the ministry don't begin in the pulpit!

Do you want to be used by God? How do you think your career in ministry is going to start? Do you think God is going to hand you the pulpit out of the clear blue and say, "There you go — now *preach*!" You'd better pray it doesn't happen that way, because you won't be ready!

Ministry begins by setting up chairs, sweeping the floors, cleaning the restrooms, etc. God doesn't promote people instantly; rather, He requires that they go through a period of training and discipleship first. The leader must watch a person's life and work with him. Then as the person proves himself faithful, the leader can slowly bring him, little by little, into more responsibility.

Faithfulness is an absolutely vital quality to look for when choosing people for promotion in ministry or in any other arena of life.

First Corinthians 1:27 and 28 says, "But God hath chosen the *foolish* things of the world to confound the wise; and God hath chosen the *weak* things of the world to confound the things which are mighty; and *base* things of the world, and things which are despised, hath God chosen...."

> **Faithfulness is an absolutely vital quality to look for when choosing people for promotion in ministry or in any other arena of life.**

These verses say that God chooses the *foolish*, the *weak*, and the *base* — or what others might consider of little value. So if you belong to Jesus, you can know that you fall into one of these categories. You are either *foolish*, *weak*, or *base*. *These are the words that describe those whom God calls!*

The word "foolish" comes from the Greek word *moraino*, from which we derive the word "moron," which could describe *someone of lower natural intelligence*. The word "weak" is the Greek word *asthene*, which nearly always describes *someone so weak that he is failing of strength*. Finally, the word "base" comes from the Greek word *agenes*, meaning *shameful* or *ugly*.

You see, none of us is really qualified to serve the Lord. God doesn't call us because of our natural gifts; He calls us because our hearts are right.

If a person's heart is right and *willing* to be taught, this "faithful man," or woman, can become much more than he or she currently is. That is why Paul said, "...faithful men, *who shall be able*...." Again, this word "able" in Greek is the word *hikanos*, which conveys the idea of *sufficiency*. Paul was basically saying, "*Timothy, they may not be the cream of the crop in the world's eyes, but you work with them. Start where they are, and develop them. Faithful men can become sufficient for the task! They are not able to do the job now, but they will be able to do it soon!*"

You can choose the most unqualified person around — but if he's faithful, he will soon be qualified! He may be a garbage collector right now, but if he is faithful, in time this person will become *transformed*. What a miracle and joy it is to see a believer raised up *through faithfulness* into a public position where he then starts teaching God's Word!

WHAT DOES THIS HAVE TO DO WITH THE COMBAT ZONE?

If you've been badly burned — misused or abused by someone close to you — you know the hurt that follows. However, this doesn't mean you should put up a wall and stop making friends.

We need fellow believers in our lives who are also our *friends*! However, the Bible says that when we make friends, we should look for "faithful" people who have *proven* themselves genuine and have shown themselves to be truly committed to the Lord and to us.

When you've been betrayed or abandoned by someone close, you must obey Paul's command in Second Timothy 2:2 and renew your pursuit of developing close relationships once again. You must become *para* with new, faithful people. In other words, get alongside them and stick close to their side for the sake of relationship and discipleship. They need more than your words; they need your *example*.

> You can choose the most unqualified person around — but if he's faithful, he will soon be qualified!

You may have been hurt in the combat zone. But the only way you'll ever obey Paul's command in this verse is to open your heart to God, ask for His assistance, and "lay hold of a steady current of God's power, which comes to you as a result of God's grace."

In Second Timothy 2:3, Paul continued, saying, "Thou therefore endure hardness, as a good soldier of Jesus Christ." In the next chapter, we will look at the necessary preparation and mental attitude you *must* have to successfully live and *win* in the combat zone.

CHAPTER FOUR

LEARNING TO ENDURE

*A*s we've seen, Timothy was facing a horrible predicament at the time Paul wrote his second epistle to him. Timothy's "combat zone" was *real, imminent,* and *deadly.*

Satan was infuriated that Jesus had been raised from the dead! With all of his fury, the enemy released the powers of hell against the Church. At times even children who professed to know Christ were killed for their faith. Yet the gates of hell did *not* prevail against the Church!

Throughout the first three centuries of the Church's existence, this type of tension between authorities and Christians was intermittently manifested in a variety of repressive and often brutal ways across the Roman Empire.

We can get an idea of the way Roman authorities viewed Christians from an exchange of correspondence written during the early Second Century between Emperor Trajan and a governor named Pliny. In the letter, Pliny was grappling with knowing how to deal with Christians, asking the emperor such questions as, "Shall I punish *boys* and *girls* as severely as grownups? Is just being a Christian enough to punish, or must a true violation of Roman law actually be committed? If the accused says he is not a Christian, should I let him go?"[6]

---

[6] Pliny, *Letters,* X.96-97.

It is my practice, my lord, to refer to you all matters concerning which I am in doubt. For who can better give guidance to my hesitation or inform my ignorance? I have never participated in trials of Christians. I therefore do not know what offenses it is the practice to punish or investigate, and to what extent. And I have been not a little hesitant as to whether there should be any distinction on account of age or no difference between the very young and the more mature; whether pardon is to be granted for repentance, or, if a man has once been a Christian, it does him no good to have ceased to be one; whether the name itself, even without offenses, or only the offenses associated with the name are to be punished.

Meanwhile, in the case of those who were denounced to me as Christians, I have observed the following procedure: I interrogated these as to whether they were Christians; those who confessed I interrogated a second and a third time, threatening them with punishment; those who persisted I ordered executed. For I had no doubt that, whatever the nature of their creed, stubbornness and inflexible obstinacy surely deserve to be punished. There were others possessed of the same folly; but because they were Roman citizens, I signed an order for them to be transferred to Rome.

Pliny also mentioned what he had heard about Christians and their "detrimental" influence on the people's worship of pagan gods. He wrote:

Those who denied that they were or had been Christians, when they invoked the gods in words dictated by me, offered prayer with incense and wine to your image, which I had ordered to be brought for this purpose together with statues of the gods, and moreover cursed Christ — none of which those who are really Christians, it is said, can be forced to do. These I thought should be discharged.... Others named by the informer declared that they were Christians, but then denied it, asserting that they had been but had ceased to be, some three years before, others many years, some as much as 25 years. They all worshiped your image and the statues of the gods and cursed Christ. They asserted, however, that the sum and substance of their fault or error had been that they were accustomed to meet on a fixed day before dawn and sing responsively a hymn to Christ as to a god, and to bind themselves by oath — not to some crime, but not to commit fraud, theft, or adultery, not falsify their trust, nor to refuse to return a trust when called upon to do so.

When this was over, it was their custom to depart and to assemble again to partake of food [the Lord's supper] — but ordinary and innocent food. Even this, they affirmed, they had ceased to do after my edict by which, in accordance with your instructions, I had forbidden political associations. Accordingly, I judged it all the more necessary to find out what the truth was by torturing two female slaves who were called deaconesses. But I discovered nothing else but depraved, excessive superstition....

The contagion of this superstition has spread not only to the cities but also to the villages and farms. But it seems possible to check and cure it. It is certainly quite clear that the temples, which had been almost deserted, have begun to be frequented, that the established religious rites, long neglected, are being resumed, and that from everywhere sacrificial animals are coming, for which until now very few purchasers could be found. Hence it is easy to imagine what a multitude of people can be reformed if an opportunity for repentance is afforded [and the threat of death given as the alternative — author's note].

AN EARLY CHURCH LEADER WHO ENDURED

One of the most famous examples of Christian martyrdom is that of Polycarp, the beloved, elderly bishop of Smyrna. Polycarp was 86 years old when he was killed in 155 or 156 AD. His martyrdom occurred more than 100 years after the death and resurrection of Jesus and illustrates how the poisonous fervor against Christians didn't subside with time but actually increased at times during the rule of certain Roman emperors.

An ancient account of Polycarp's martyrdom relates the events leading up to his arrest and execution.[7] As the story goes, during a huge gathering of pagans, a hate-filled mob began screaming, *"Away with the atheists!"* (Remember, pagans called Christians atheists because believers in Jesus refused to burn incense to pagan gods.)

As this unruly mob began to rant and rave against the city's believers, a person yelled, *"Get Polycarp!"* The bloodthirsty crowd soon took up this cry, and an order went out to seize Polycarp and bring him before the mob. When Polycarp heard the news, he wanted to surrender because he was not afraid of death, but his fellow believers beseeched him to hide in the country. Polycarp agreed to hide out of love for his loyal friends, but despite their well-meaning efforts, Polycarp was discovered and taken into custody shortly after he retreated to the countryside.

When Polycarp was brought before the mob and put on trial, a sympathetic proconsul tried to persuade Polycarp to renounce Christ and thus save his own life. But Polycarp adamantly refused, "Eighty and six years have I served Him, and He has done me no wrong, and can I revile my King who saved me?"

The governor insisted again, *"Swear by Caesar! I'll throw you to the beasts if you do not!"* The old bishop answered, "Bring on the beasts!"

The governor quickly replied with indignation, *"If you scorn the beasts, I'll have you burned!"*

---

[7] *Epistle of the Smyrneans.*

Polycarp looked the governor straight in the eyes and said, "You try to frighten me with the fire that burns for an hour, and you forget the fire of hell that *never* goes out."

Infuriated by Polycarp's boldness, the governor yelled to the crowd, *"Polycarp admits he is a Christian!"* The crowd went wild, hollering and shouting. They screamed, *"This is the teacher of Asia, the father of Christians, the destroyer of our gods!"*

The crowd then got huge bundles of wood and placed them around the feet of the faithful bishop. As the fire began to swirl around him, tradition says that Polycarp prayed loudly:

> **O Lord God Almighty, Father of Jesus Christ… I bless Thee that Thou didst deem me worthy of this hour, that I shall take a part among the martyrs in the cup of Christ and to rise again with the power of the Holy Spirit. May I be an acceptable sacrifice…. I praise Thee. I bless Thee. I glorify Thee through Jesus Christ…. Amen.**

Total Commitment
in the Face of Opposition

This historical account paints a clear picture: Early Christians had a *very* intense "combat zone" to deal with. They didn't have padded pews, cushioned chairs, stained-glass windows, Christian radio and television stations, and Bible bookstores. To be a Christian in the First Century literally meant *total commitment in the face of great opposition.*

It's difficult for believers in modern Western society to comprehend the horrific tribulation their brothers and sisters in the Early Church endured. Even so, the greatest crisis early believers faced was *not* the persecution itself, but rather the substantial number of *defections* that took place as a result of that persecution.

If you look back at Pliny's letter to Trajan, you find a clear mention of these mass defections from the Church. Pliny wrote, "...The temples, which had been almost deserted, have begun to be frequented, that the established religious rites, long neglected, are being resumed, and that from everywhere sacrificial animals are coming, for which until now very few purchasers could be found."

As Pliny's assertion reveals, a number of Christians were reverting to paganism in order to save their lives!

Persecution revealed the *genuineness* of a believer's faith. Sadly, many people forsook the Lord, deserted the Church, and went back to their old ways. It is likely that Timothy saw this take place in his own church — and to his dismay, he may have even witnessed it among his *leaders*. Some of those who were called to help Timothy instead told him in essence, *"See you later, Pastor! We're out of here until the heat dies down!"*

In the midst of this turbulent environment, it's understandable that Timothy may have felt completely isolated. Many of the men and women he thought were his friends had left his congregation out of fear. Perhaps they didn't want to be associated with Timothy or the church any longer. This was a very, very tough time for Christians.

Since this is likely what happened, Timothy definitely could have had a grudge to bear. From a natural standpoint, he had every right to hold a grudge, be upset, and feel hurt. Every feeling he had was seemingly justified.

There are times when we feel that we have a right to hold a grudge — but the truth is, holding grudges will always do *us* harm. Grudges, anger, animosity, unforgiveness, and contempt do nothing but bring ruin and destruction in our lives.

Timothy had a reason to be hurt. However, he couldn't give place to that hurt and still be victorious — *and neither can we*. It's far too deadly. That's why Paul's exhortation in Second Timothy 2:1 is so important: "Thou therefore, my son, be strong in the grace that is in Christ Jesus."

> Timothy had a reason to be hurt. However, he couldn't give place to that hurt and still be victorious — *and neither can we*. It's far too deadly.

WHEN YOU'RE WOUNDED IN A CHRISTIAN RELATIONSHIP

When the Lord Jesus spoke to the seven churches of Asia in Revelation 2 and 3, He was speaking to churches that had major problems. For example, Ephesus was backslidden and had lost its first love; Pergamum held to the deceptive doctrine of the Nicolaitans; Thyatira had a woman named Jezebel in its congregation who was seducing church members; Sardis was spiritually dying; and Laodicea was lukewarm.

Don't these sound like "troubled churches" to you? Each of these congregations had some very serious problems. Yet despite all of their shortcomings, Jesus still called them "*golden*"! When Jesus explained the symbolism of the vision to John in Revelation 1:20, He said, "...The seven [*golden*] *candlesticks* which thou sawest are the *seven churches.*"

From man's perspective, these churches probably didn't look golden at all. In fact, most of them looked like they were on their way to spiritual bankruptcy! Yet Jesus looked at them in all their mess and still saw them as unique and precious.

We must never forget that Jesus shed His blood for the Church. Even with all the problems in the Christian community today, He still loves His Church. We must learn to love it just as Jesus does. *It is His Body!*

If you have been wounded by brothers and sisters in Christ, you must forgive them. If it seems like you are unable to forgive, you must seek God to *learn* to forgive them.

In moments when you feel angry and disgusted with others in the Church, you have to remind yourself — *Jesus still loves His people.* Despite all the obvious problems and blemishes in the modern Church, Jesus still looks at His people and calls them *"golden."*

> We must never forget that Jesus shed His blood for the Church. Even with all the problems in the Christian community today, He still loves His Church.

However, many Christians who have experienced hurt or betrayal from those who are part of the Church are like a person who has wounded himself by accidentally ramming his arm through a glass window. Obviously, an injury like that would hurt pretty badly. In fact, he'd probably rush to the emergency room to see if any tendons or major blood vessels had been severed and to have the doctor stitch up his arm.

But let me ask you this: Just because that person's arm is stitched up, does that mean his arm is immediately ready to be used again? Of course not. If he's not careful, he'll rip those stitches loose — and he may find himself back in the emergency room having his wound stitched up again.

This can be likened to being wounded in a relationship. Just like physicians, your dear friends surround you to check you out and make sure your thoughts and heart are centered on the Lord.

Then they help "sew you up" with their love and care so you can heal from the emotional wounds.

To get back out into the middle of the fight and place yourself in jeopardy before you are properly healed would be foolish. You need healing. And that's all right. However, it *isn't* all right to take advantage of your situation in order to avoid your responsibilities.

Some people have avoided church for years because of an incident that occurred 30 years earlier. Throughout the decades, they have held on to their hurts, grudges, resentments, and unforgiveness. They've told their "horror story" a thousand times, displaying their wounds for all to see as a reason they should never again get involved with another church.

Are you going to let Satan do that to you?

As long as we are on this earth, we will live in the combat zone — and as a result, we'll sometimes be wounded by a surprise attack. It's not fun, but we must recognize this as a possibility. Sometimes it just happens! Even good soldiers are taken by surprise at times.

It's true that we should equip ourselves to deal with future attacks through prayer, study, meditation, praying in tongues, faith, consecration, attending church, etc. However, we must make a determined decision that if we're ever blindsided by something hurtful that others do or say, we will immediately forgive and allow the Holy Spirit to begin working in our hearts. That way we can be healed and restored as soon as possible so we can return to the front lines of battle where we're called to fight.

This is why Paul exhorted Timothy, "Thou therefore, my son, be strong...." Again, the word "strong" is the Greek word *endunameo,* which speaks of *an inner strengthening or empowering.* Specifically, it refers to *a deposit of power in the inner man.*

God's power will hasten your healing process.

There is no need for you to sit around and hurt for weeks, months, or years to come. God's power is available to take care of your problems. With that kind of current flowing through you, it won't take long before you're ready to get up and jump back into the action!

> We must make a determined decision that if we're ever blindsided by something hurtful that others do or say, we will immediately forgive and allow the Holy Spirit to begin working in our hearts.

Getting back on your feet might seem a little scary to you at first if your wounds are still very fresh in your mind. But don't let that keep you from taking that all-important step. Just know that it was uncomfortable for Timothy too! That's why Paul said in Second Timothy 2:3, "Thou therefore endure hardness, as a good soldier of Jesus Christ."

ENDURING HARDNESS AS A GOOD SOLDIER OF CHRIST

When Paul wrote those words in Second Timothy 2:3, he used four particular Greek words that conveyed a very strong message to Timothy — and to us! Particularly notice the phrase "endure hardness" and the words translated "good," "soldier," and "of." These words are all extremely important.

First of all, Paul said, "Thou therefore endure *hardness....*" What does this word "hardness" mean? In the Western world, most people haven't had to deal with much "hardness." Only a small proportion of the population has actually fought for their nation and knows the effects of war. For the most part, people live in nice homes or apartments and have reliable transportation.

And if they don't, these amenities are accessible to most if they desire them enough to truly work for them.

Because of their material blessings, most people in the Western world haven't had to deal much with "hardness." They may have to work overtime for seasons at a time, or they may have their vacation time or other benefits cut — and that might seem "hard." They may have to live in a house with old carpet or drive an older car, both of which can seem like major inconveniences for different reasons. Or sometimes they may have to mow their own yard, which to some might seem rather "hard."

In general, that's the nature of our modern Western society. For the most part, people have little or no knowledge about *real* hardship in their culture. And if someone preaches on "enduring hardness," many don't like that preacher very much. They might even start looking for another church!

This is a major reason why the Church of Jesus Christ is producing so little power in this hour. "Hardness" to many Christians might mean having to get to church on time after a busy week. Or it may seem to some like they're "enduring hardness" when the pastor preaches too long and cuts into their lunch plans, or when they're asked to serve as volunteers in an area of the church that isn't their preference. The truth is, the concept of commitment has been greatly diluted in modern times.

Don't get me wrong — I'm thankful for the way God has blessed believers in the Western world. However, the typical "I'll do it if it's easy" attitude of many in this country has negatively impacted the spiritual commitment of many Christians. If things get tough, they don't resolve to stay put and fight where God has called them to fight. Instead they say, "Well, if it's *hard,* it must not be God. If it was God, it would all just fit together nicely with no problems because when He does something, it just falls into place!"

Try telling that to the Christians of the First, Second, and Third Centuries — or to the Christians *today* who live persecuted lives in other areas of the world. Most of them would never think of saying, "I'll live for Christ if it's easy." *They know the real meaning of a life commitment.*

HOW THE CHURCH CONTINUED STRONG
FOR GENERATIONS

Satan hates the Church. He wants to keep it torn up, divided, messed up, confused — and full of people who run away when things get "hard."

Had the believers of those early centuries taken a lackadaisical approach to their walk with God, the Church of Jesus Christ wouldn't have gotten very far! *Those early believers were more committed to their task than their oppressors were to theirs.* The early Christians knew what their mission was in the world. They defied Satan as well as the Roman emperors who persecuted them mercilessly — *and they outlasted them all.*

> **Satan hates the Church. He wants to keep it torn up, divided, messed up, confused — and full of people who run away when things get "hard."**

We need to thank God that these early believers weren't "wimpy" in their commitment to the faith. If only the modern Church was that committed today! It's sobering to imagine how many Western Christians would defect from the Church if we were subjected to the same persecution those early believers experienced.

To many Western believers, Christianity simply means getting together once a week to sing songs, raise their hands, politely hold hands with their neighbors during prayer, give their weekly or monthly offering to the Lord, listen to a nice sermon, shake hands with the pastor, and wave at everyone as they drive off to eat their Sunday afternoon lunch with family or friends. Many think they can enjoy God without personal cost or having to pay any price.

However, despite the prevalence of this type of fair-weather Christianity, there also exists a contingent of deeply committed spiritual warriors who boldly stand their ground for the Kingdom of God. It's so powerful when you find a church that is genuinely committed! Their songs are filled with *war*! Their sermons are loaded with *conviction, challenge,* and *a call to a higher commitment.*

In a committed church, believers walk away *confronted,* knowing what God is requiring of them. When God speaks to these congregations, His voice echoes loudly like the voice of a Commander! In these churches, sickness is healed; bondages are removed; sin is dealt with; slothfulness is shunned; and weak, wimpy, "don't-make-it-too-hard" thinking is non-existent. *These saints view themselves as enlisted in the ranks of God's army.*

This warfare mentality was the kind of thinking required to survive the combat zone of the First Century — and it's the kind of thinking Christian soldiers need today in order to impact the modern world!

Take Your Place in the Ranks

As we saw earlier, Paul advised Timothy in Second Timothy 2:3, "Thou therefore endure hardness, as a good soldier of Jesus Christ." To conquer the crisis he was facing, Timothy had to possess a *warfare mentality.*

Notice again that Paul said, "...Endure hardness...." This phrase in Greek tells you something very important about doing the work of the Lord. If you're experiencing a difficult struggle as you obey God concerning your personal life, your healing, your marriage, your finances, or your church, this applies to you.

The phrase "endure hardness" is the Greek word *sunkakopatheo*, which is actually three different words compounded into one word. These three Greek words are *sun*, *kakos*, and *pathos*. Because this phrase is composed of three different words, it actually conveys *three distinct ideas*. Although the translation "endure hardness" is technically correct, it doesn't adequately reveal the full depth of meaning contained in the compound word *sunkakopatheo*.

This compound Greek word was carefully selected by the Holy Spirit! The first part of the word *sunkakopatheo* is the Greek word *sun*, which denotes *cooperation, connection,* or *partnership*. This little word *sun* always connects a person to someone else.

There are many examples of this word found throughout Scripture. For example, in Second Corinthians 6:1, it says, "We then, as *workers together with him*...." This phrase "workers together with him" is derived from the Greek word *sunergo*, which is a compound of the words *sun* and *ergo*. As we just saw, the word *sun* conveys the idea of *connection* or *partnership*, and the Greek word *ergo* refers to *a worker*. When compounded, these two words describe *two or more partners working together on the same job*.

In other words, we aren't working for the Lord by ourselves. Rather, we are coworkers with God, cooperating with Him in our work. This is not merely a figure of speech. God is with us, doing the same job at the same time. *He's literally working together with us as a Partner.* This is exactly what the Bible means when it says that we're "workers together with him." It's a description of our partnership with God.

But let's go back to the phrase "endure hardness" (*sunka-kopatheo*) in Second Timothy 2:3. The first part of that Greek compound word is *sun*, which, as we saw in the two previous examples (*see* 2 Corinthians 6:1), is used to convey the idea of *partnership*. The second part of the compound word *sunakopatheo* is the Greek word *kakos*, which is a very familiar Greek word. It's used most often in Scripture to convey the idea of something that is *wicked, foul, bad* or *evil*.

If all you had were these first two words, *sun* and *kakos*, they would mean *become a partner with this vile, wicked, horrible, foul situation.* However, Paul went further and used a third Greek word, *pathos*. The third part of the compound word *sunakopatheo* is *pathos*, another well-known Greek word. It normally describes *suffering*.

You may ask, "What does suffering have to do with being a good soldier of Jesus Christ?" *A lot!* The Greek word *pathos* is very important for Christian combat fighters!

You see, this word was perfectly suited for Timothy's situation. Timothy was suffering in many ways as a result of the stressful situation he found himself in — and he knew he could even suffer physically in the very near future. This is another reason why Paul's words in Second Timothy 1:7 were so vital: "For God hath not given us the spirit of fear; but of power, and of love, and of a *sound mind*."

Have you ever been in such an intense situation that you thought your mind was going to "break"? Have you ever been pushed up against a wall so hard that you thought you might have a nervous breakdown?

What if you knew that the government had your name and planned to torture and kill you? What if you knew that they weren't going to tell you when they were going to arrest you and take you away? You would be tempted to think and think and *think* about it until eventually it began to affect your mind!

For those who are blessed to live in the Western world, this may seem like an unrealistic example, but it wasn't for Timothy. Nero was killing many believers with a vengeance, and Timothy knew his number could be up soon too! He may have wondered which method of death they might use on him. Would they burn him, stone him, hang him, crucify him, or fillet him with a knife?

Timothy must have wondered what it felt like to die a martyr's death. Every time someone knocked on the door of his house, Timothy may have wondered if it was the Roman authorities coming to arrest him. It would be very understandable to be overwhelmed, subdued, and negatively affected by such a situation.

That is why Paul admonished Timothy to "endure hardness," using the three words *sun*, *kakos*, and *pathos*. When compounded, these Greek words mean: *"Join in as a partner with the rest of us* (sun) *who are soldiers for the Lord; face the vile, horrible, foul, ugly circumstances* (kakos) *that are all around you; and if you must, suffer* (pathos) *to get the job done!"*

There were several key messages to Timothy in this word. First, Paul was telling Timothy that he wasn't the *only* soldier serving the Lord. Although it might have looked to Timothy like everyone else had abandoned the Lord, this wasn't the case. Many believers were, in fact, still faithful. Therefore, Paul essentially said, *"You're not in this mess alone. Your problems are not unique! A bunch of us are facing the same dilemma right now. Rather than running away from it, join in with the rest of us combat-zone soldiers!"*

Second, by using the word *kakos*, Paul was telling Timothy, *"Yes, you're right. It's getting pretty bad out here in the combat zone! This is a bad, foul, wicked situation we're facing right now."* This was a good message for Timothy to hear because he needed to know that he wasn't the only one facing trouble.

Third, Paul told Timothy to "suffer" if he must. Paul knew what it was like to suffer, and he didn't want to believe that on anyone! However, a job needed to be done, and if it meant suffering to get it done, then suffer he must.

Every Christian soldier who is committed to taking ground for the Kingdom of God must have this mentality.

WHAT IS A GOOD SOLDIER OF JESUS CHRIST?

When Paul said, "Endure hardness," he was laying it on the line to Timothy, making it clear what is required of a soldier in the Lord's army.

Paul was saying, in essence, *"Timothy, you're not the only one who has been wounded on the battlefield. The rest of us have too. Quit thinking you're the only one who's ever been through hardship, and join in with the rest of us who are faithfully fighting it out. You must come to grips with the horrible situation around you. It doesn't look like it's going to change soon, and, in fact, it might get worse before it gets better. Instead of living the remainder of your life in fear, rise to meet the occasion! Face your fears, and if necessary, suffer to get the job done that God has called you to do. Suffering is no fun, but someone must do the job. Even if your mind is under great stress, keep doing your ministry anyway."*

Paul continued talking about this warfare mentality in Second Timothy 2:3 by saying, "...Endure hardness, as a *good* soldier...." This word "good" is very important. In Greek, it's the word *kalos*, which describes something that is *good, beautiful, fine, excellent, fit, capable,* or *virtuous.* By using this word, Paul wasn't just describing an ordinary soldier; he was describing *an excellent soldier, a fine soldier*, or *a soldier who was fit, capable, or beautiful*.

The soldier Paul described possessed all the correct "virtues" that a Roman soldier should possess. This describes a good soldier. We'll discuss the full training, requirements, and virtues of a Roman soldier in Chapter Six.

Keep in mind that Paul was writing in a day when the Roman Empire had conquered much of the known world. Thus, to use this symbolism was very significant. The "virtues" of Roman soldiers were well known. They were skilled, disciplined, committed, fierce, driven, and hard-working men.

Throughout the New Testament, Paul used *military* language to refer to himself, his friends, and the Church at large. By using this kind of terminology, Paul told Timothy what God *expects* from him, from us, and from every member of the Body of Christ.

Those who desire to be a leader in the Body of Christ must know that their assignment will set them apart from other people. Although the layperson is very much involved in the battle, leaders in the Church are subject to attack more frequently than those who are simply part of the congregation. Satan knows the important, strategic place in the Church held by the fivefold ministry, so he never stops working his diabolical plan to destroy every apostle, prophet, evangelist, pastor, and teacher he can reach. He knows that if he can hit a leader and knock him or her out of the battle, he can wound a significant part of the Body of Christ with one blow!

We are in the midst of a raging war, and the apostle Paul understood this. That's why he used militaristic language to describe our spiritual life.

And the early believers understood that kind of language. They had a very militaristic view of themselves, believing that they were to "take" the world until every nation had been evangelized and converted to the knowledge of Jesus Christ.

So sure were early Christians of their mission that they literally changed their world and the course of history for all time. They didn't sit around and wait for another wave of the Spirit before they rose up in power. They had *already received* power. They knew what Jesus wanted them to do, and they *did* it. In order to accomplish their mission, they were willing to sacrifice everything.

> So sure were early Christians of their mission that they literally changed their world and the course of history for all time.

Paul often spoke of being "a good soldier of Jesus Christ." Throughout his epistles, he referred to himself as a soldier; he referred to Timothy as a soldier; and he even referred to Jesus as a soldier.

Notice the word "of" in Paul's phrase "a good soldier *of* Jesus Christ." This little world could actually be translated *like*. Paul was really saying, *"Be a good soldier like Jesus Christ."* Jesus Christ was a Soldier!

Paul was very militaristic in his commitment to the Lord. He cut no slack for his flesh at all. Paul knew he had been called of God, and he was going to do *whatever was required* in order to finish the job God had called him to do.

This militaristic mentality was reflected in nearly all of Paul's relationships and his epistles. For instance, in Romans 16:7, he greeted the saints in Rome with military language. Instead of simply saying, "Tell the saints in Rome hello for me," like we would today, Paul said, *"Salute* Andronicus and Junia, my kinsmen, and my fellowprisoners...."

Does this sound like "regular" church talk to you? When you enter the door of your church on Sunday, do you salute those inside the building? How many times have you called yourself "the prisoner of the Lord"? Do you hear that kind of talk when you go to church?

Paul's words did *not* fit in the category of allegorical speech. He was actually "saluting," or expressing strong respect for, others who were fighting a real battle on the front lines! Many of them were physically imprisoned because they had courageously preached the Gospel of the Kingdom of God. They were enduring persecution because of their faith and the political connotations that accompanied their beliefs.

The message of the Kingdom of God was highly controversial and political in nature. It *demanded* allegiance to a higher Power, a higher King, and another Kingdom. Because of this, the early Christians, including Paul, were truly suffering for the Gospel — just like soldiers who had been captured by hostile forces.

This was the language of the New Testament Church. Persecution and warfare were *realities* for them. The early believers never had the privilege of simply being "church people." Neither did they view themselves simply as a congregation. *They believed they were the army of the Lord.*

THE *GREAT* COMMISSION

When Jesus gave the Early Church the Great Commission, the believers of that day took it seriously. In Matthew 28:19 and 20, Jesus said, "...Go ye therefore, and teach all nations, baptizing them in the name of the Father, and of the Son, and of the Holy

Ghost: Teaching them to observe all things whatsoever I have commanded you...."

Couple Matthew 28:19,20 with Jesus' words in Acts 1:8, which says, "But ye shall receive power, after that the Holy Ghost is come upon you: and ye shall be witnesses unto me both in Jerusalem, and in all Judaea, and in Samaria, and unto the uttermost part of the earth." You discover that the Early Church really believed they were to take the entire earth for Jesus Christ — not just *affect* it. *They were committed to take the world.*

When I was growing up, I thought — like many Christians — that this verse meant, *"Try* to go into all the world. *If you can,* send missionaries to *some parts* of the world. Although it's really not possible to win them all, *try* to win *some* in every nation. Of course, it will never happen, *but give it your best shot* to bring the Good News to every segment of society."

Do you know what we've done? We've taken the "Great Commission" and turned it into the "Little Commission"! Our thinking says, "Go into every nation and try to win *some*, if possible." What's "great" about that kind of a commission? That isn't what Jesus intended!

Jesus doesn't intend for us to "reach just a few people" in every country or to send missionaries to "just a few places" in every country. The intention of Jesus was that we, His Church, would rise up so strong in the Spirit and so militant in our faith that we could literally reach the entire world and give *every member* of *every nation* the opportunity to be a disciple of the Lord Jesus Christ.

The Early Church believed in a *worldwide conversion,* and they gave their lives to see it happen. They knew the whole world needed Jesus Christ!

The parallel verse for Acts 1:8 is Psalm 2:8, which says, "Ask of me, and I shall give thee the heathen for thine inheritance, and *the uttermost parts of the earth* for thy possession." Early believers were asking for *that*. They saw themselves as an *army* advancing to take *the world* for Jesus Christ!

> We've taken the "Great Commission" and turned it into the "Little Commission"! Our thinking says, "Go into every nation and try to win *some*, if possible."

The early New Testament Church had a militaristic mentality. Believers were absolutely committed to the faith. They were going to turn the world upside down and take it for Jesus Christ. And to see this vision realized, they gave their lives for their cause. Some early Christians were thrown in jail; and some were killed. Yet they continued to defy Satan and outlast numerous Roman emperors. *They did, in fact, change the world forever!*

The early Christians viewed themselves as a militant Church. However, the weapons of their warfare were "not carnal" (*see* 2 Corinthians 10:4). Second Corinthians 6:6 and 7 reveals that their weapons worked by "...pureness, by knowledge, by longsuffering, by kindness, by the Holy Ghost, by love unfeigned, by the word of truth, by the power of God, by the armour of righteousness on the right hand and on the left."

Fully equipped in spiritual armor, the early Christians were driving back the forces of hell! Therefore, it was logical for them to use military language when they spoke to one another. That is why Paul began his greeting in Romans 16:7 with the word *"Salute."*

In Romans 16:9-16, Paul continued to salute many other fellow warriors in Christ. He wrote:

1. *"Salute* Urbane...and Stachys...."

2. *"Salute* Apelles...."

3. *"Salute* Herodion...."

4. *"Salute* Tryphena and Tryphosa...Persis...."

5. *"Salute* Rufus...."

6. *"Salute* Asyncritus, Phlegon, Hermas, Patrobas, Hermes...."

7. *"Salute* Philologus, and Julia, Nereus, and his sister, and Olympus...."

8. *"Salute* one another...."

It's almost as though Paul was saying, *"Tell my comrades hello for me. I salute them!"* Imagine how powerful the Church would be today if we had this same type of thinking! This is still God's plan for the Church today.

WHERE ARE THE FRONT LINES?

Do you see why Paul's mind thought militaristically? He lived and fought in the combat zone! That's why he told Timothy to be "a good soldier of Jesus Christ." Timothy was fighting on the front lines!

You may ask, "Where are the front lines of battle today?"

The battle occurs wherever God has told you to take a stand of faith. It is certain that this is precisely where Satan will show up to resist you. When you take a stand of faith and put your knowledge to work, that's when the battle really begins and the devil starts throwing darts at your life!

It's easy to read a book on healing or to listen to an audio teaching on prosperity. The battle begins when you start *obeying* the Word. That is when the enemy comes to attack. That is your battleground.

You'll have every opportunity to pack your bags and split the scene. There will be times when you'll want to look for greener grass elsewhere. It always looks so good on the other side of the fence — *until* you get there. Once you're there, however, you find out it's the very same.

God has called you and me to fight *right where we are.* We are to take the land *where we are.* And if it gets tough where we are, we must join with other brave spiritual warriors to face the reality of opposition, overcome it, and get the job done — even if it causes our lives to be temporarily uncomfortable.

The battle occurs wherever God has told you to take a stand of faith. It is certain that this is precisely where Satan will show up to resist you.

You are called to be tough. You are called to endure. You are called to face all opposition with courage! Therefore, you must commit to joining in with the other soldiers and fighting until the battle is over and won.

This is extremely important for us to understand if we're going to live as overcomers in the combat zone. This kind of thinking is *required* on our part. That's why Paul told Timothy, *"Endure hardness, and join with the others who are fighting. Face the vile circumstances, and if it means you must suffer, then suffer. You must do whatever it takes to get the job done!"*

A verse that all believers need to know is Proverbs 28:19 (*NIV*), which says, "Those who work their land will have abundant food, but those who chase fantasies will have their fill of poverty."

Let's look closer at this verse: "He that works his ground will have abundant food; but the man who chases [*runs here and there, never sticking with any commitment, job, or church*] after fantasies [*strange ideas and daydreams that are not founded on scriptural principles*] shall have his fill of poverty."

There is a principle in this verse that we need to hear and apply to our lives: *If you stay right where God has planted you and work the ground, you're going to eventually produce a crop.* It might take time, but the harvest *will* come.

If you're chasing every little whim and notion that comes along all the time, you won't produce anything of real value for the Kingdom of God. Instead, you will waste your life chasing after dreams and fantasies of your own making.

> If you stay right where God has planted you and work the ground, you're going to eventually produce a crop. It might take time, but the harvest *will* come.

We're all hungry and ready for a new, supernatural move of the Spirit. However, running here and there isn't a picture of stability! Ephesians 4:14 says, "That we henceforth be no more children, tossed to and fro, and carried about with every wind of doctrine...."

We must get in the army of God, fight the battle where we are, and "work our ground."

The truth is that when God calls you to do something difficult, your mind tends to drift to other things. And if you aren't truly committed to doing what God told you to do, you'll be tempted to think that your drifting mind is the leading of the Spirit.

Nothing that changes this lost world and drives back Satan's forces is easy. My wife and I learned this early on in the ministry.

By the late 1980s, our teaching ministry had grown quickly. And *then* came God's call in 1991 for me to move my family to the former USSR!

If I had allowed my mind to drift during those challenging years, it would have been happy to comply. I would have found it so easy to daydream about other places where life was easier and beautiful landscapes were filled with tall mountains, sweet-smelling pines, and fresh snow. However, I knew I could *never* fulfill God's plan for my life if I didn't deliberately make myself focus on what He has called me to do.

JUST WHEN YOUR BREAKTHROUGH IS ABOUT TO OCCUR

The temptation to get distracted by thoughts that pull you off track usually comes when you're on the brink of an incredible breakthrough. God is getting things in alignment in your life, and hell's forces are being driven back. But then the pressure becomes so intense that you give in to fear and decide to slip away to try your "luck" elsewhere.

> *God is looking for combat-zone fighters* — those who will stay steadfast at their assigned post and fight the good fight of faith until Satan's works are demolished and their assignment has been fully executed.

It can be *very* difficult to "endure hardness." Don't let anyone convince you otherwise. The devil hates what you're attempting to do in your city, your ministry, your business, or your family. He can't bear the thought of you bearing fruit or of God winning *another* victory through your life!

That's why it's critical for believers to determine that they *will* "endure hardness." *God is looking for combat-zone fighters* — those who will stay steadfast at their assigned post and fight the good fight of faith until Satan's works are demolished and their assignment has been fully executed.

This is why Paul's words to Timothy were so pivotal for the younger minister's life. Timothy was scared and hurt. He was afraid that he might be murdered! Timothy understood what Paul's words meant.

- If staying true to what God has asked you to do means facing vile situations, *then face them.*

- If it means you have to suffer, *then suffer.*

- If it means martyrdom, *then face martyrdom.*

- If God has called you to pastor, *then pastor.*

- If God has called you to travel and teach, *then travel and teach.*

- If God has called you to evangelize, *then evangelize.*

- If God has called you to prophesy, *then prophesy.*

- If God has called you to do apostolic work, *then do apostolic work.*

- Whatever the assignment is that God has given you, *get the job done.*

You may ask, "Rick, doesn't this demand a great deal of us?" Yes, it does. *It will require our very lives.* That is the decision that lies before each of us: *Will we choose to follow Heaven's Commander-in-Chief and give our lives to becoming "good soldiers of Jesus Christ"?*

CHAPTER FIVE

ANOTHER NEW TESTAMENT SOLDIER WHO ENDURED

*E*veryone has had to "endure hardness" at some point in his or her life. In Second Corinthians 1:8 and 9, Paul described in great detail the hardness he endured in Asia. There he wrote, "For we would not, brethren, have you ignorant of our trouble which came to us in Asia, that we were pressed out of measure, above strength, insomuch that we despaired even of life: But we had the sentence of death in ourselves, that we should not trust in ourselves, but in God which raiseth the dead."

Notice Paul's wording in the first part of verse 8: "For we would not, brethren, have you ignorant of our *trouble* which came unto us in Asia...." This word "trouble" is the Greek word *thlipsis*, and it's especially important because it paints a vivid picture of the kind of hardship Paul endured. In ancient Greek literature, this word *thlipsis* was used to convey the idea of *a heavy-pressure situation*. It depicts a person who is *in a tight place*, *under a heavy burden*, and *in a great squeeze*.

By using this word *thlipsis*, Paul was essentially saying, *"We were under an unbelievably heavy amount of stress and pressure. We were beneath a heavy load and trapped in very tight circumstances! Our minds were being squeezed, and it felt like the life was being pushed right out of us."*

At first glance, one might think Paul was referring to *physical suffering* in this verse. However, he was most likely referring to *mental suffering*. Pain in the body is difficult, of course, but the greatest suffering always occurs in the mind. In fact, people can endure debilitating pain in their bodies if they still have control over their minds. However, when suffering begins to work on the mind, the body will break and fold.

Second Corinthians 1:8 reveals that Paul's greatest suffering in Asia was not physical, but *mental*. This is made apparent in his next statement, where he said, "…We were *pressed out of measure*, above strength, insomuch that we despaired even of life." Particularly pay heed to the phrase "pressed out of measure." This is the Greek phrase *kath huperbole*, which literally means *to throw something beyond*. It can also describe something that is *excessive* or *beyond the normal range that most experience*.

By using this phrase, Paul was saying, *"We were under an abnormal amount of pressure. It was far beyond anything we had ever previously experienced. It was excessive, unbelievable, unbearable, and far too much for any one human being to endure."*

Paul continued to describe his pressing situation by using the phrase "above strength." This word "above" is important as well. It's the Greek word *huper*, which always conveys the idea of something *excessive*. It's almost as though Paul was saying, *"Normal human strength would never have been sufficient for this situation. This predicament required strength on a measure that I had never previously needed. It was beyond me!"*

Then Paul said in verse 8, "…insomuch that we *despaired* even of life." The Greek word for "despaired" is the word *exaporeomai*, which was used to describe *a situation with no way out*. In fact, it's where we get the word "exasperated." This is a word used to describe individuals who were *caught, pinned down, trapped, up against the wall, and utterly hopeless.* In today's language, one might say, *"Well, sorry, but it looks like this is the end of the road for you!"*

Paul went on to say in verse 9, "But we had the *sentence* of death in ourselves...." The word "sentence" in Greek is the word *apokrima*, which in this sense speaks of *a final verdict.* What Paul meant was, *"It looked to us like the verdict was in, and we were not going to survive. The verdict was death for us and, in fact, that is what we were already experiencing in ourselves at that time. We felt the verdict of death already operating in our souls."*

When the meanings of all these different words and phrases are combined in this context, it becomes very plain that Paul's primary suffering at this moment was *mental*, not physical. He was describing mental agony on a measure few of us will ever know.

In fact, this passage could be translated:

"We would not, brethren, have you ignorant of the horribly tight, life-threatening squeeze that came to us in Asia. It was unbelievable! With all the things we've been through, this was the worst of all — it felt like our lives were being crushed. It was so difficult that I didn't know what to do. No experience I've ever been through required so much of me. In fact, I didn't have enough strength to cope with it. Toward the end of this ordeal, I was so overwhelmed that I didn't think we'd ever get out! I felt suffocated, trapped, and pinned against the wall. I really thought it was the end of the road for us! As far as we were concerned, the verdict was in, and the verdict said "death." But really, this was no great shock, because we already were feeling the effect of death and depression in our souls...."

What happened to cause so much mental stress in Paul's life? His friends forsook him! He faced death every day — *and this is not a figure of speech.* He *literally* faced the prospect on a daily basis of experiencing a grueling, horrible death.

That's why Paul said in verse 8, "We would not, brethren, have you *ignorant*...." You may ask, "Why did Paul want us to know about this? Did he want people to feel sorry for him?"

Absolutely not! Paul wanted believers to know that everyone must endure hardness from time to time. *Even great spiritual leaders are confronted with potentially devastating situations that they must overcome for the sake of the call.*

With all of Paul's knowledge, revelation, and experience, he still *almost* broke down. This conclusion isn't just *my* idea about Paul; it's what he himself said in this verse. When Paul wrote, "...We despaired even of life," he was describing the most excruciating kind of mental pressure imaginable!

But this apostle didn't break, and he didn't die! And if *you* remain committed to fighting right where you stand, *neither will you.* Just like Paul, you'll win the victory and be able to say you came through that experience with the assurance that you will not trust in yourself, "...but in God which raiseth the dead: Who delivered us from so great a death, and doth deliver..." (2 Corinthians 1: 9,10).

God's delivering power is yours! He will rescue you now, and He will rescue you again and again in the future. All He asks is that you stay there at your post, refuse to give in to pressure, refuse to let the devil win, and enforce the victory Jesus won for you. If you remain faithful to your task, God will remain faithful to you as well.

GOD'S SOLDIER ON A BARREN ISLAND

Now that we've looked in greater detail at how Paul persevered for the Gospel, let's look for a moment at another great example in Scripture of a man who endured incredible hardness — the apostle John. This story begins many years after Nero died when another demonically inspired emperor named Domitian gained control of the Roman Empire. Domitian's persecution of the Church was even more intense than the war against Christians that had been waged by Nero.

Just like Nero, Domitian hated Christians. However, by the time Domitian came to power, all of the apostles had been martyred except for the elderly apostle John. So when Domitian learned that John was the last remaining apostle, the emperor arrested John and shipped him to Rome to stand trial for his faith.

> *God's delivering power is yours!* **All He asks is that you stay there at your post, refuse to give in to pressure, refuse to let the devil win, and enforce the victory Jesus won for you.**

Tradition relates that Domitian ordered John to be dipped into a big vat of boiling oil. The devil wanted to make John's death a hideous one! However, God's hand of protection was on John, and when he emerged from the scalding oil, there wasn't a single burn or scratch on his body.[8]

Needless to say, Domitian was infuriated — so he exiled John to a small island in the middle of the Mediterranean Sea. The island of Patmos was noted for its rocky terrain and forbidding weather. The island of Patmos was also one of Rome's repositories for murderers, robbers, and criminals of every kind.

At the time of John's exile, he was an old man whose only crime was that he had faithfully served the Lord for many decades. Yet

---

[8] Tertullian, *Prescription Against Heretics*, c. 36.

it appeared that John would finally meet his death on this barren island.

We can gain a more in-depth understanding of John's attitude in the midst of this crisis by studying Revelation 1:9. It says, "I John, who also am your brother, and companion in tribulation, and in the kingdom and patience of Jesus Christ, was in the isle that is called Patmos, for the word of God, and for the testimony of Jesus Christ."

Notice how John described himself in this verse. His description is very important because it reflects the mentality of a *great combat-zone fighter*. John identified himself with four distinct descriptions — a *brother*, a *companion in tribulation*, a *companion in the kingdom*, and *a companion in patience*.

First and foremost, John wrote, "I John, who also am your *brother.....*"

Why did John introduce himself as "a brother"? There is more in this word than first meets the eye. You may say, "Well, John called himself a brother because he is a Christian." Yes, that's true. But there is more to this statement than that.

By using this word "brother," John conveyed a specific message to other believers who were suffering just like he was. Essentially he was saying, *"Not only am I your brother in a spiritual respect, but I am your brother in affliction, in persecution, in problems, in struggles, and in trials. You and I, we are the very same — we are brothers."*

You may ask, "Rick, why is John's self-identification as a brother so important?" It's important because some people think that great spiritual leaders have such refined faith that they avoid all hardships. But this is an absolutely false perception. Great spiritual leaders experience hardship just like everyone else.

The great apostle John found himself on the island of Patmos, suffering as a criminal. Yet he didn't want sympathy — he wanted to encourage the saints. He wanted them to know that they were not alone in their predicament!

There is something else found here in Revelation 1:9 that is very important. Notice how John *didn't* introduce himself. He didn't say, *"I, John, the great, illustrious, powerful, anointed, special, well-known apostle of Jesus Christ...."* As a contemporary father in the faith and the last of the original disciples of Jesus Christ, John could have made those statements in all honesty, but he didn't. Why *didn't* he say these things?

You see, when you're in the heat of battle fending off satanic attacks from all sides, popularity and celebrity status cease to matter. Affluence, prestige, power, and notoriety all lose their importance when you're living in the combat zone. In fact, you forget all about such things.

When John wrote those words, it didn't really matter at that moment that he was *John, the beloved disciple of Jesus*. All people, whether well known or unknown, feel the same pain, hurt, and confusion, and they all experience the same struggles in life.

> **When you're in the heat of battle fending off satanic attacks from all sides, popularity and celebrity status cease to matter.**

Next, John went on to state the key ways in which he was experiencing brotherhood and unity with other saints. He began by saying, "I John, who also am your brother and *companion in tribulation...."*

This word "companion" is the Greek word *sugkoinonos*, which is a compound of two Greek words, *sun* and *koinonos*. The first word, *sun*, conveys *partnership*.

The second part of the word, the Greek word *koinonos*, speaks of *a common experience, something that everyone experiences*, or *something that is shared*. When these two words are combined into the word *sugkoinonos*, it describes *two or more persons who are joined in partnership and are sharing the same experience together.*

It's very significant that John used this particular Greek word. Once again, he was removing the "awe" from who he was by saying, *"I am your brother. In fact, you and I are partners together in this ordeal. What you're experiencing, I'm experiencing too. We're sharing a common experience. We're in this together!"*

What John was experiencing through persecution, others were experiencing as well. At that time, persecution was a very sharp reality for all believers. *They were all living and fighting in the combat zone.*

However, John didn't stop there. He continued by saying, "I John, who also am your brother and companion *in tribulation.…*"

This word "tribulation" in Greek is the word *thlipsis*, which is the same word Paul used to describe his difficult circumstances in Second Corinthians 1:8. Again, this Greek word conveys the idea of *a very heavy load, a burden that is crushing; being pinned against the wall; being pushed to the limit;* or *being forced to bear a load far too heavy for any individual to bear.*

Hearing John call himself a "companion in tribulation" (*thlipsis*) was also good news for the other believers. You see, all early believers shared this testimony. They were forced to carry an excessively heavy burden. Life was difficult, hard to bear, and nearly crushing. Therefore, John said to them, *"I understand what you're going through. I am your brother and fellow partner in these crushing difficulties."*

Why was it important for other believers to hear that John was experiencing difficulties? It was important because he was a leader, the *only* remaining apostle first chosen by Jesus, and now a very old man. *The apostle John was their primary example.*

If John could endure in his old age, the other believers knew they could endure as well. If John remained true, they knew they could remain true too. They needed to hear victory in his words, and that is *exactly* what they were hearing through his writings to them.

Then John went on to add something else very important. He said, "I John, who also am your brother and companion in tribulation, and in *the kingdom*...."

This mention of "the kingdom" is of vital importance because it tells us that John never forgot his most important identity. While the world viewed him as a political rebel and a maverick and imprisoned him as a criminal, John was still very aware that he was *a member of God's Kingdom*. It was for this Kingdom and the Gospel of the Kingdom that John was suffering. With all the persecution that had come against him, John had taken none of it personally. He knew the world wasn't really against him — *it was against the Kingdom he represented.*

Although John was *suffering* for this Kingdom, he knew that the Kingdom *rewards* were also his! And although he was indeed "a companion in tribulation," he knew that he must keep a *proper perspective* of things.

The real issue wasn't John; *it was the Kingdom.* John and his brothers and sisters in Christ all had to keep this in the forefront of their thinking. They had to be willing to pay *any price needed* to see this Kingdom advance to reach a lost world. John was happy to be a soldier for the Kingdom of God, and he was proud to be a political prisoner on behalf of his King.

Then John mentioned something else extremely important in verse 9. He said, "I John, who also am your brother, and companion in tribulation, and in the kingdom and *patience* of Jesus Christ...."

Notice especially this word "patience." It's from the Greek word *hupomeno*, which is a compound of two Greek words, *hupo* and *meno*. The word *hupo* refers to *being underneath something*. In this case, it's a picture of *being underneath something very heavy*. The word *meno* literally means *I stay*, and it describes *a decision to abide in one spot and not move away from it*. Combined, these two words describe *the resolute decision of someone who is determined to stay in one spot, even if the load gets excessively heavy*. Personally, I like to translate *hupomeno* as *staying power* or *hang-in-there power*.

Patience (*hupomeno*) was considered to be the queen of all virtues by the Early Church. If a person had *hupomeno*, he or she could endure any trial and last longer than any adversary. All early believers aspired and prayed to have this virtue because they knew that if they had it, they would *always* win!

By using this word, John made his point clear. He was essentially saying, *"Just like the rest of my brothers and sisters, I am under an unbelievably heavy load — a load so heavy it should crush me — but I have decided not to move! I know the Gospel is true. I know what Jesus Christ has done in my own life. And I am NOT going to move off my stance of faith in Him!"*

In the end, John's "patience" even caused him to outlive his persecutor, Domitian! *Ultimately those who endure always win in the combat zone.*

John continued in Revelation 1:9, explaining *why* he was in Patmos. He said, "I...was in the isle that is called Patmos, for the word of God, and for the testimony of Jesus Christ."

It might seem incredibly unfair to put an old man on a barren island, intending for him to die there "…for the word of God, and for the testimony of Jesus Christ." However, it didn't matter whether John's situation was just or unjust; it was happening regardless. The important thing was that John dealt with it correctly, endured it like a good soldier, and *came out a winner.*

If you're going through a difficult time, this principle applies to you as well. You may be tempted to think, *How did this happen? What did I do wrong? Why did God allow this to take place? How did I let Satan get in and do this to me?* But your questions won't change your situation. What's important is that you deal with the devil's attack bravely, endure hardness if you must, and come out of that combat zone a winner!

> **Ultimately those who endure always win in the combat zone.**

Don't budge an inch. Don't give in to the devil's attacks! Stay in the place God has called you to. *Refuse to be moved,* even if the load seems as if it has become too much for you to bear. Patience and endurance will put you over and put Satan under! *Satan has no counterattack for patience!*

JOHN'S REWARD FOR HIS FAITHFUL ENDURANCE

In the midst of John's trying circumstances — *in the middle of his combat zone* — something wonderful happened to him. He had a personal visitation from the King! And what a visit it was! John received a special touch from the Lord during that divine visitation to encourage him, to keep him pursuing the plan of God, and to let him know that the King for whom he was suffering knew of his plight.

In Revelation 1:10 and 11, John went on to write, "I was in the Spirit on the Lord's day, and heard behind me a great voice, as of a trumpet, saying, I am Alpha and Omega, the first and the last...."

Notice John said, "I was in the Spirit on the Lord's day...." Two things are important to see about this testimony. First, John said, "I was in the Spirit." Second, he mentioned a specific day called "the Lord's day." Both of these phrases carry great weight and significance. Why? Because they tell us *how* this visitation took place, *what* John was probably thinking about when it took place, and *why* it took place on "the Lord's day."

When John said, "I was in the Spirit," the word "was" is the Greek word *ginomai*, which is very important. This word *ginomai* indicates that John didn't know this experience was about to occur. This visitation with Jesus took the elderly apostle completely by surprise. *He wasn't expecting it at all!*

The word *ginomai* was often used in Scripture to describe *something that occurs unexpectedly*. For example, in Acts 10:10, it's used to describe how Peter's vision took place. There the Bible says, "And he became very hungry and would have eaten: but while they made ready, *he fell into a trance.*" This phrase "he fell into" is the Greek word *ginomai*, and it tells us Peter wasn't expecting to have a vision that afternoon. He was simply on top of the roof, praying and waiting for dinner, when — *ginomai!* — he slipped into a trance.

The idea of *ginomai*, as used in Acts 10:10, indicates that Peter *fell into* a trance, *slipped into* a trance, or *unexpectedly found himself* in a trance. The idea conveyed is that this vision took Peter by surprise.

Going back to Revelation 1:10, we see that John used the same word to describe the events he experienced in Patmos. Essentially

John meant, *"I don't know how it happened. I was not expecting this to occur. I looked up, and to my astonishment, I had stepped out of this realm and over into the realm of the Spirit."* This vision was unexpected and took John completely by surprise.

Thus, the word *ginomai* tells us *how* John's visitation took place. Suddenly — *out of nowhere* — he was transported into the realm of the Spirit. He hadn't been praying for a special visitation or wishing for an angel to appear. He was simply doing what he had to do to survive every day on that barren island when suddenly *the Lord Jesus Christ appeared before him.*

What exactly was John thinking when this awesome visitation took place? The key is found in verse 10 in the phrase "the Lord's day."

The "Lord's day" is *not* what it seems at first. At first glance, it might appear that John was talking about the Sabbath or perhaps the first day of the week when believers gathered to worship the Lord. But both of these assumptions are wrong. The "Lord's day" mentioned in this text is actually a definite reference to *paganism* and *emperor worship*. It is translated from the Greek word *kuriakos*, which was used in a technical sense to describe *a day that was set aside by the emperor primarily for the sake of emperor worship.*

In Roman times, this day was called "the Imperial Day," and it was nearly always associated with the practice of emperor worship. On this day, citizens of the Roman Empire were expected to worship the emperor and burn incense in his honor.

On the very day when the people of the Roman Empire were worshiping their demented emperor, there came an appointed moment on the desolate island when Jesus Christ — the *true* King and Lord over everything — came to see His great soldier, John. The King for whom John was "enduring hardness" had come to reveal Himself in all of His *majesty, power, and might!*

When Jesus revealed Himself to John in that instant, He was dressed *in the clothing of an emperor* — wearing a gold imperial sash around His chest and kingly garments down to His feet. His feet were as fine brass that had been burnished in a furnace (*see* Revelation 1:13,15).

John was immediately awestruck at Jesus' appearance and overwhelmed with Jesus' magnificent Lordship. No doubt he was flooded with the thought, *O Jesus, You are my King!* It didn't matter that the entire Roman Empire was worshiping a demon-possessed man on that same day — Jesus was still Lord over all! And on this "Lord's day," He came to reveal Himself to a spiritual warrior who had paid a very, very high price. By appearing in the regal attire of an emperor, Jesus was saying to John, *"Yes, John, I am the true Emperor."*

John related this experience in Revelation 1:12-18:

> **And I turned to see the voice that spake with me. And being turned, I saw seven golden candlesticks; and in the midst of the seven candlesticks one like unto the Son of man, clothed with a garment down to the foot, and girt about the paps with a golden girdle. His head and his hairs were white like wool, as white as snow; and his eyes were as a flame of fire; and his feet like unto fine brass, as if they burned in a furnace; and his voice as the sound of many waters.**
>
> **And he had in his right hand seven stars: and out of his mouth went a sharp twoedged sword: and his countenance was as the sun shineth in his strength. And when I saw him, I fell at his feet as dead. And he laid his right hand upon me, saying unto me, Fear not; I am the first and the last: I am he that liveth, and was dead; and, behold, I am alive for evermore, Amen; and have the keys of hell and of death.**

What a visitation! The apostle had paid a high price, enduring persecution and great hardness for the sake of the Gospel. But then Jesus revealed Himself to John *in the midst* of his excruciating circumstances.

Let's look at the words that Jesus, our Great Emperor, used as He spoke to John in verse 18. He said, "I am he that liveth, and was dead; and, behold, I am alive for evermore...." Notice the first part of that statement, which reads, "I am he that liveth, and *was dead...."* The phrase "was dead" in the original Greek would actually be better understood, *"I became temporarily dead...."* This is significant because it describes to us how Jesus views His own experience of "enduring hardness" on the Cross.

Although Jesus' death on the Cross was hellish in nature, it was but a brief interruption in His ongoing, eternal existence. The first part of Revelation 1:18 can be translated as saying, *"I am He that liveth, but once I became dead...."*

Jesus was addressing John, a combat-zone fighter who had endured much hardness. Jesus' proclamation of His victory over death must therefore have provided great encouragement to John's heart! John must have thought, *Yes! Jesus, You completely understand my situation. You, too, have been through hardness!*

However, the Lord didn't stop there. He continued, "...And, behold, I am alive for evermore...." Just as death was not able to stop Jesus Christ, neither were the forces of hell going to stop John. Although John's situation was dire, it was merely a brief interruption — *a temporary setback.* King Jesus was about

> **Just as death was not able to stop Jesus Christ, neither were the forces of hell going to stop John. Although John's situation was dire, it was merely a brief interruption — *a temporary setback.***

to bring John out of the horrible pit and back to his spiritual family once more.

How the Lord Comes to Us

John was suffering as a soldier; therefore, he needed to hear an encouraging word from *his* "Emperor." Jesus knew exactly how to come to John. He knew that John needed to know that the King and the Kingdom for which he was "enduring hardness" were aware of his plight.

Perhaps you also find yourself struggling in a difficult situation. If so, Jesus is eager to reveal Himself to you in a way that is tailored to your specific need.

- If your problem is sickness, Jesus Christ will reveal Himself as *the Great Physician*.

- If your problem is mental affliction, Jesus Christ will reveal Himself as *the Great Deliverer*.

- If your problem involves a conflict in your church, Jesus Christ will reveal Himself as the great *Head of the Church*.

- If your problem is financial, Jesus Christ will reveal Himself as *the Great Provider*.

Through the centuries, just as John and others endured "hardness" as good soldiers, God expects *you* to endure the temporary hardness that life brings at times. Just entrust yourself to the Lord, and stand fast in your commitment to do what He asks, no matter what. As you do, you will not only win those battles, but you will also gain a brand-new perspective of Jesus Christ that will call you higher and make you stronger in Him.

CHAPTER SIX

WARRING IN
THE COMBAT ZONE

*T*hus far, we've seen that Paul had been speaking to Timothy using military language. In Second Timothy 2:3, Paul told Timothy to "endure hardness" and then called the young pastor "a good soldier of Jesus Christ." This militaristic mindset is pervasive throughout Paul's writings. In fact, spiritual warfare and fighting as a good soldier of Jesus Christ are common themes that run throughout all the Pauline epistles. Paul was serious about fighting and winning the war in the combat zone!

In Second Timothy 2:4, Paul continued to use militaristic language in order to convey his message to Timothy. He wrote, "No man that warreth entangleth himself with the affairs of this life; that he may please him who hath chosen him to be a soldier." In this verse, Paul employed four significant words and a specific phrase that clearly liken our spiritual commitment to that of Roman soldiers — and the *best* Roman soldiers at that!

First, let's look at the word "warreth." The word "warreth" is the Greek word *strateuomenos*, which was a word that described *a soldier's function*. What was a soldier's function in Roman times? First and foremost, it was to be in the practice of *warring, fighting, killing,* and *conquering*. In addition, a soldier's function also referred to the intense training that was required of every Roman soldier, including constant drills, military exercises, and deliberately imposed hardships.

The average Roman soldier was fully and regularly immersed in all the disciplines that accompany warfare.

Keep in mind that at the time Paul penned his epistles, Rome had already conquered much of the known world with its great armies. Thus, to use explicitly militaristic language in that day and age would definitely convey a specific image to the reader. What would come to mind almost immediately would be scenes of *skilled, disciplined, driven, committed, hardened, physically fit warriors.*

Nearly everyone who lived in the Roman Empire knew about the lifestyle of Roman soldiers. It was a rigorous way of life, filled with constant training and exercise. This lifestyle was intended to take a normal man and make him into a good man, to take a good man and make him into a great man, and to take a great man and make him into a nearly perfect man. Roman soldiers never stopped striving for perfection. *They were committed 100 percent!*

Because Paul used the illustration of a Roman soldier to convey his message about commitment and spiritual warfare, let's take a look back in time to see what the ancients recorded about the life of a Roman soldier.

THE ROMAN SOLDIER IN NEW TESTAMENT TIMES

Flavius Vegetius Renatus (commonly known simply as Vegetius) was a high-ranking Roman who wrote the most influential surviving document on Roman warfare. Although it is generally accepted that Vegetius lived and wrote in the late Fourth Century AD, more than 300 years after the death of Paul, his writings describe military practices that in many ways had remained unchanged since New Testament times. Vegetius' knowledge of First Century Roman military practices was extensive and unrivaled by any contemporary.

Woven throughout Vegetius' words is found the full backdrop of what Paul meant when he called Timothy a "good soldier of Jesus Christ." We can also discover the reason Paul wrote to believers in verse 4, "No man that warreth entangleth himself in the affairs of this life; that he may please him who hath chosen him to be a soldier."

At the time Vegetius wrote his document, entitled *Concerning Military Manners*, the armies of Rome had become lax, uncommitted, and unprepared for war, and the majority of the soldiers had become weak, physically out of shape, untrained, and lazy. Instead of viewing their opportunity to serve in the military as a privilege, soldiers saw their station in society as a nasty, uncomfortable, unwanted obligation.

Vegetius sought to rectify this deteriorating situation by studying the successful armies of Rome's past. He diligently searched through ancient records to glean whatever strategies or advice he could find. Finally, when he had completed his exhaustive research, Vegetius distilled what he learned into a comprehensive treatise that clearly outlined the essential qualities of a strong and successful army. This seminal work would become widely revered and used as a guidebook for the Roman military for centuries to come.

Sadly, in many ways, the modern Church has slipped into a state of deterioration that echoes the Roman armies of Vegetius' day. Because many believers today have grown up in a period of peace and prosperity, the army of God has become lax. To a great degree, the Church is unprepared for war, despite all of its knowledge and teaching. Far too many believers have become weak-willed, untrained, spiritually fat, and lazy. Instead of viewing their walk of faith as a privilege, they see it as an uncomfortable, unwanted obligation.

> **Because many believers today have grown up in a period of peace and prosperity, the army of God has become lax. To a great degree, the Church is unprepared for war, despite all of its knowledge and teaching.**

When Paul told us to endure as "a good soldier of Jesus Christ," he specifically used the Roman soldier of his day as an illustration to teach us how we need to live and fight in the combat zone. Therefore, we can look to Vegetius' military document to draw an accurate analogy between Roman warfare in the First Century and our own spiritual warfare. As we continue, we will see many principles in Vegetius' writing that are direct applications to our own life in the combat zone.

THE PERFECT SOLDIER

Let's look at the qualities of the men whom Vegetius said made the best recruits for the Roman army:

> ...The peasants are the most fit to carry arms for they from their infancy have been exposed to all kinds of weather and have been brought up to the hardest labor. They are able to endure the greatest heat of the sun, are unacquainted with use of baths, and are strangers to the luxuries of life. They are simple, content with little, inured to fatigue, and prepared in some measure for a military life by their continual employment in their country-work, in handling the spade, digging trenches, and carrying burdens.[9]

---

[9] Vegetius, *Concerning Military Manners*, I.ii.2.

Vegetius asserted that peasants made the best soldiers for seven specific reasons:

1. They were accustomed to extreme weather.

2. They were used to hard work.

3. They could endure heat.

4. They lived simple, uncomplicated lives.

5. They were content with having little.

6. They were immune to fatigue.

7. They were already accustomed to such physical labor as digging and carrying burdens.

Why did these qualities make a man better suited for service? Why were these qualities so vital when it came to selecting the best soldiers? Let's examine these seven characteristics individually to find out how they make the best kind of soldier.

The first characteristic that Vegetius said made peasants the best soldiers was that they had been "exposed to all kinds of weather." Warfare takes a soldier through all manner of weather and temperatures — storms, cold, rain, snow, sleet, etc. Yet as unbearable as these outward conditions might seem to the soldier at the time, *the war must go on*. Therefore, a good soldier must be able to push forward and tolerate any kind of weather in order to accomplish his goal.

Likewise, when you begin fighting your fight of faith, the weather of life can change on you without any prior warning! Satan knows exactly when to cause some bad events to blow into your life and bombard your mind with a spine-chilling report. It seems that one of his favorite tactics is to cause great climatic changes in your environment as soon as you make a step of faith.

However, these temporary shifts in weather do not change the *reality* of your fight. When the sun disappears, the winds begin to blow, and the sleet begins to fall, you must keep fighting your fight of faith anyway! Don't allow Satan to scare you off to some other, more comfortable zone. Although it may look like the stormiest season of your life, the weather won't last long. If you are true to the fight, you will outlast the storm!

The second reason Vegetius said peasants made the best soldiers was that they had been "brought up to the hardest labor." Why was this trait important? Because combat will involve the most difficult work imaginable! If a soldier was afraid of hard work, he would cringe at the first sign of struggle.

Likewise, if believers are afraid of hard work, they will never get one thing done for the Kingdom of God. *As combat-zone fighters, they must be willing to do the hardest type of work on a sustained basis — all for the cause of Christ.*

> **Although it may look like the stormiest season of your life, the weather won't last long. If you are true to the fight, you will outlast the battle!**

Third, Vegetius said that peasants "are able to endure the greatest heat of the sun." It could get scorching hot on the battlefield. Therefore, a soldier needed to be able to push through the discomfort and endure the heat till the battle was won.

In the same way, it can get very "hot" on the battlefield when you're dealing a deathblow to the devil's strongholds. He'll fight you all the way to the end! Therefore, as a soldier in God's army, you need to be ready to *"take the heat."*

Fourth, Vegetius wrote that peasants made good soldiers because they were "simple." Simple does not mean "stupid" in this context; rather, it means "uncomplicated." You see, the best soldiers are simple and uncomplicated. They are free from care, anxiety, worry, and personal ambitions. They are free to do their job without any type of reservation. To be a good soldier is their sole aspiration in life.

Just as this kind of single-mindedness always marks the best soldiers in the natural realm, the same is true for spiritual warriors. The best combat-zone fighters are those who live unfettered, uncomplicated lives. They are solely dedicated to their mission to serve the Lord, and they don't let *anything* get in their way of fulfilling what God has asked them to do.

Fifth, Vegetius said peasants made the best soldiers because they were "content with little." This statement was not meant to imply that Roman soldiers should embrace a life of abject poverty. Rather, Vegetius was saying that the best soldiers are people who don't *require* a great deal of comfort and unnecessary amenities. That was why peasants were so good at warring. Life had never afforded much luxury to them, so they weren't even aware they were missing anything!

Sometimes when the blessings of God come into our lives and our financial resources begin to grow, we can lose sight of where we came from. And as we adapt to our new, higher level of prosperity and blessing, we forget the fight of faith we waged in order to get there. However, as good soldiers of Jesus Christ, we must never allow the blessings of God in our lives to knock us out of the *combat* zone into the *comfort* zone. *Even in peacetime, we must be willing to pay any price to win new territory for the Kingdom of God.*

The sixth reason peasants made good soldiers, according to Vegetius, is that they were "inured to fatigue." This phrase refers to *a willingness to keep working, fighting, and warring even when a person feels like he or she has been pushed to the limit.* You see, peasants didn't have the privilege of saying, "I've done all I can do today, and I'm tired, so I'm going to stop working." They had to *work* until the job was finished and their master was satisfied.

Strong armies are composed of warriors who are willing to go the extra distance in order to get the job done — soldiers who are "inured to fatigue." Thus, Roman military commanders sought to enlist soldiers who would *stretch* and *push* themselves and press forward, even when their flesh screamed, "No!"

Likewise, when you are waging war against the forces of hell, *endurance* is the name of the game. You won't lose your fight in the combat zone because you don't have enough power or authority. As a child of God, you automatically have far more power and authority than the devil. But there *is* something that has the power to knock you out of the fight, and that is a lack of endurance to stay in the battle and keep warring with the weapons of your spiritual warfare (*see* 2 Corinthians 10:5,6)!

If you can endure, you'll win the battle. Satan's tolerance for losing in every showdown with you will inevitably wear out. He'll recognize that you have endurance, and he'll know that he can't beat you. His only option will be to bow out and leave the fight. And when the devil retreats, everything that you've been working and praying for will come to you so quickly that it will seem like a miracle! But in actuality, it won't be a miracle at all; it will be the direct result of your willingness to stand your ground, fight back, and endure. If you had given up earlier in the fight, you never would have received those blessings from God.

Finally, we come to the seventh trait on Vegetius' list. He asserted that peasants are best fit to be soldiers because they are accustomed to "digging trenches and carrying burdens." The armor and weaponry of a Roman soldier was very heavy. In order to effectively wage warfare, the soldiers had to be able to dexterously wield their weapons and move quickly about the battlefield if they hoped to survive the fray. This required men who were physically strong and not intimidated by the prospect of carrying a heavy load. Each soldier needed to be able to carry his own weight and, if the situation called for it, help share the burden of an injured comrade. There was no room for wimps in the Roman army!

Like it or not, the load of ministry and spiritual warfare can get very heavy. If we are wimpy and afraid to carry a little extra weight, we can kiss our vision and our victory goodbye forever!

These seven traits are essential qualities for good combat-zone fighters. Peasants may not have been the intellectuals of their day or members of the high-ranking aristocracy. However, their hard-working existence in the field prepared them to be the best of fighters.

The upper crust of society — the pampered aristocracy — knew nothing of hardship, hard work, fatigue, unbearable cold or heat, digging trenches, or carrying burdens. If a spade had been placed in their hands, they wouldn't have known what to do with it!

Furthermore, when you examine the history of the Early Church, you find that the majority of the early Christians were not nobility; they were just regular people. They were exactly the kind of people Vegetius described — unspoiled by the luxuries of life, content with little, inured to fatigue, and accustomed to hard work — and they were the very ones whom Paul called "faithful men." They were, in fact, perfect soldiers in the army of the Lord!

> When the devil retreats, everything that you've been working and praying for will come to you so quickly that it will seem like a miracle! But in actuality, it won't be a miracle at all; it will be the direct result of your willingness to stand your ground, fight back, and endure.

In First Corinthians 1:26-28, Paul wrote, "For ye see your calling, brethren, how that not many wise men after the flesh, not many mighty, not many noble, are called: But God hath chosen the foolish things of the world to confound the wise; and God hath chosen the weak things of the world to confound the things which are mighty; And base things of the world, and things which are despised, hath God chosen, yea, and things which are not, to bring to nought things that are."

Paul knew the background of the Roman army. He knew that it was primarily composed of individuals from the poor, uneducated lower class. If it were not for the army, those soldiers would have remained peasants, poor and unimportant in the eyes of society. However, once they enlisted and committed their lives to a greater cause, they commanded people's respect. They made the best soldiers because they knew how to fight!

It is a similar situation in God's spiritual army. The majority of people who answer God's call are not from the intellectual or aristocratic elite; rather, they are those whom the world would never recognize. These brave men and women hold a place of deep respect in His Kingdom because they have committed their lives to the cause of Christ.

Vegetius also wrote, "It is certain that the less a man is acquainted with the sweets of life, the less reason he has to be afraid of death."[10] You see, people who have had to struggle in life often make the best combat-zone fighters. This is because they have nothing to lose and everything to gain! For them, the risk of failure is almost zero. In the world's eyes, they are already failures, but in God's eyes, they are shining examples of success. Because they aren't afraid of damaging their reputation or losing their station in life, there is nothing holding them back from answering the Lord's call and entering the fight to further His Kingdom on the earth.

---

[10] Vegetius, *Concerning Military Manners*, I.ii.3.

THE CREAM OF THE CROP

In his military document, Vegetius also wrote, "In choosing recruits, regard should be given to their trade. Fishermen, fowlers, confectioners, weavers, and in general all whose professions more properly belong to women should, in my opinion, by no means be admitted into the service. On the contrary, smiths, carpenters, butchers, and huntsmen are the most proper to take into it."[11] Basically, Vegetius was saying, *"The rougher the background, the better the fighter."*

Many times over, I've heard believers say, "I really lived for the devil before I got saved. I did a lot of bad things and made a lot of rash decisions. I don't think there is any way God would want to use a person like me. I have had a pretty rough background."

Believe it or not, your rough background may just make you one of the best combat-zone fighters!

So what if your life was rough before you found Christ? Now you know the Lord. Take the same vigor you used to serve the devil, and use it now to serve the Lord. *You may rise to become the cream of the crop!*

Vegetius continued, "But what good can be expected from a man by nature a coward, though ever so well disciplined or though he has served ever so many campaigns?"[12] Highbrow training, education, social status, and family lineage are not synonymous with courage. The truth is, some of the greatest cowards in the midst of an intense battle can be the soldiers who are considered trained, educated, and elite!

Cowards have no place in the army of God. There are many instances in the history of the Church in which God has raised up

---

[11] Vegetius, *Concerning Military Manners*, I.vi.1.
[12] Vegetius, *Concerning Military Manners*, I.vi.2.

profoundly uneducated people to do His will because they were willing to take the risk.

So take heart! Even if your previous experience as a fighter was in the world before you accepted Christ, you may be one of the most qualified warriors to do battle in the spiritual combat zone. All it takes is your willingness to fight in the strength of the Lord.

THE BEST AGE FOR ENLISTING

Concerning the best age for enlistment, Vegetius wrote, "The proper time for enlisting youth into the army is at their age of puberty. At this time, instructions of every kind are more quickly absorbed and more lastingly imprinted on the mind. Besides this, the indispensable military exercises of running and leaping must be acquired before the limbs are too much stiffened by age. For it is activity improved by continual practice which forms the useful and good soldier."[13]

> You may be one of the most qualified warriors to do battle in the spiritual combat zone. All it takes is your willingness to fight in the strength of the Lord.

In this passage, we find an excellent example of the difference between God's wisdom and man's reasoning. Man would say, "Leave the young boys at home. They are not ready for such instruction. They are too young to be used." However, God purposefully seeks to use young men and women in His combat zone to accomplish great things in His name!

One of the best examples of God calling young people to do the work of the ministry is the story of Jesus choosing His

---

[13] Vegetius, *Concerning Military Manners*, I.iii.1.

12 disciples. Jesus called young men because He knew that they were malleable and that His instruction could more readily be absorbed into their hearts. The traditions of men had not yet set into their souls, and they were *young enough* and *bold enough* to take the necessary leap of faith to lay down everything familiar in their lives and follow Him.

Vegetius wrote: "The indispensable military exercises of running and leaping must be acquired before the limbs are too much stiffened by age."[14] That also applies to people's spiritual walk. Too many people who chose to ignore God's calling when they were young found it to be very difficult to move forward later in life because their spiritual limbs had stiffened through years of neglect and disuse.

Let this be a wakeup call to you. It's crucial that you RESPOND when God calls you!

That is why Paul told Timothy, "Let no man despise thy youth..." (1 Timothy 4:12). The Bible is full of instances in which God called young people to rise up as spiritual warriors and change their world. For example, Samuel was just a child when he was established to be a prophet for all of Israel (*see* 1 Samuel 3:20). Being young is a blessing if the person is willing to listen and be used by God.

We must never forget the principle found in Job 32:6-9 (*NIV*): "I am young in years, and you are old; that is why I was fearful, not daring to tell you what I know. I thought, 'Age should speak; advanced years should teach wisdom.' But it is the spirit in a person, the breath of the Almighty, that gives him understanding. It is not only the old who are wise, nor only the aged who understand what is right."

There are no age restrictions in God's army. He is looking only to find *yielded vessels* to accept into His ranks. Even young people

---

[14] Ibid.

can be used as mighty fighters in the combat zone if they have the breath of the Almighty on their lives!

How To Train Good Soldiers

Concerning military training, Vegetius wrote, "We find that the Romans owed the conquest of the world to no other cause than continual military training, exact observance of discipline in their camps, and unwearied cultivation of the other arts of war... They thoroughly understood the importance of hardening them [new recruits] by continual practice and of training them to every maneuver in line and in action. Nor were they less strict in punishing idleness and sloth."[15]

> There are no age restrictions in God's army. He is looking only to find *yielded vessels* to accept into His ranks.

You may be thinking, *That is incredible! They really expected a great deal out of their soldiers!* That is *exactly* the point! It was the commanders' high expectations and intense training of their troops that laid the foundation for future victory.

To a great extent, the Church at large is trying to affect a lost world without requiring any sacrificial effort from its ranks. What would happen if believers today would choose to harden themselves for spiritual battle and go through continual, rigorous training and discipline? I can tell you this — the condition of the Church's ranks would be much different.

But instead of being hard on slothfulness and undisciplined behavior, many churches choose to pamper their members. Church leaders go out of their way not to hurt anyone's feelings.

---

[15] Vegetius, *Concerning Military Manners*, I.i.2.

They make a great effort to not ask anything of their congregations that would require any extra effort on their part.

We are supposed to be the army of the Lord, but the Church today is full of complacent civilians instead of seasoned soldiers!

Concerning the need for discipline, Vegetius wrote, "No state can either be happy or secure that is amiss and negligent in the discipline of its troops."[16] He also wrote, "A handful of men, inured to war, proceed to certain victory, while on the contrary numerous raw and undisciplined troops are but multitudes of men dragged to slaughter."[17] Similarly, spiritual troops must be prepared, trained, and disciplined, or they become easy targets for the enemy's strategies to steal, kill, and destroy.

The training regiment for new recruits in the Roman army included marching, leaping, swimming, sword practice, drills, and other forms of military exercises. All of these exercises were *essential*. Only after the recruits proved their worthiness through this period of training — not only in physical and mental endurance but also in courage — did they receive "the military mark." This was a permanent mark branded by a hot iron on the hand of every soldier.

> We are supposed to be the army of the Lord, but the Church today is full of complacent civilians instead of seasoned soldiers!

About this aspect of the soldiers' training, Vegetius wrote, "Many, though promising enough in appearance, are found very unfit upon trial. These are to be rejected and replaced by better men; for it is not numbers, but bravery that carries the day. After their examination, the recruits should then receive the military

---

[16] Vegetius, *Concerning Military Manners*, I.xii.2.
[17] Vegetius, *Concerning Military Manners*, I.i.2.

mark, and be taught the use of their arms by constant and daily exercise."[18]

Too often, the Church places its official mark of approval on people before they are ready. New arrivals in a local church are often quickly elevated into positions of authority because of their outward appearance or past accomplishments. But time and time again, this practice of quick promotion has been known to result in *catastrophe*.

Paul wrote about the importance of spiritual preparation in First Timothy 3:6, saying, "Not a novice, lest being lifted up with pride he fall into the condemnation of the devil." And in First Timothy 5:22, he reiterated this point by admonishing Timothy to "lay hands suddenly on no man...."

A church must *know* its troops. If a person cannot complete the necessary training, he should not receive "the mark." If he or she doesn't submit to authority, tithe, regularly attend services, withhold his judgmental opinion, and so forth, he should never be formally recognized as a combat-zone fighter or be put in a position on the front lines in ministry.

If a person cannot follow through on basic requirements, why should you believe this person will remain true in the middle of a real challenge? Instead of promoting him prematurely, wait until his heart is softened, his soul is made ready, and he is tried and proven to be fit to be used.

MARCHING, RUNNING, LEAPING, SWIMMING!

Let's look at another powerful statement made by Vegetius: "...Troops who march in an irregular and disorderly manner are always in great danger of being defeated."[19]

---

[18] Vegetius, *Concerning Military Manners*, I.vii.1-2.
[19] Vegetius, *Concerning Military Manners* I.viii.1.

Marching in "an irregular and disorderly manner" might sound to you like an apt description of the Church in recent years. The Church's disorganization at times has certainly allowed the enemy access to implement his agenda and bring devastating blows against the Church and individual believers.

As soldiers in the Lord's army, we must understand exactly what our role is in the Body of Christ. Once we know our God-appointed place, we must make every effort to get in formation, stand firm in our proper position, and learn to march to the Lord's orders — without being threatened by the position or authority of other people. *That's when we will be able to inflict great harm upon the enemy!*

> **Once we know our God-appointed place, we must make every effort to get in formation, stand firm in our proper position, and learn to march to the Lord's orders — without being threatened by the position or authority of other people.**

In addition to marching, Vegetius wrote that Roman soldiers were taught to *run*, *leap*, and *swim*. He said, "But the young recruits in particular must be exercised in running, in order to charge the enemy with great vigor.... Leaping is another very necessary exercise, to enable them to pass ditches or embarrassing eminences of any kind without trouble or difficulty."[20]

Charging the enemy and jumping ditches — this is a description of *an aggressive and unrelenting faith*. If you've been walking with the Lord any length of time, you can probably think of a few challenging situations in your life when you've had to charge the enemy and jump a few ditches to win the victory!

---

[20] Vegetius, *Concerning Military Manners*, I.viii.2.

If you're a combat-zone fighter, you know there are times when you must face the enemy eyeball to eyeball, challenge him, and force him to move. Similarly, you know that the ditches and problems in your life often seem to appear out of the blue! It is when you are charging the enemy, jumping ditches, and scaling impossible obstacles that the mettle of your faith is put to the test.

In addition to running and jumping ditches, Vegetius also wrote that swimming was an essential exercise for any soldier. He said, "Every young soldier, without exception, should in the summer months be taught to swim; for it is sometimes impossible to pass rivers on bridges, but the flying and pursuing army both are often obliged to swim over them."[21]

Swimming across otherwise impassable rivers takes determination and sheer courage! It is a picture of "enduring hardness" and doing whatever it takes to get the job done.

Also, notice that Vegetius specifically said, "Every young soldier, without exception, should be...*taught to swim....*" This is interesting because it tells us that *these skills do not come naturally to most of us.* We must be instructed and trained in the ways of warfare if we want to succeed in battle.

> In order for the flesh to get in line and be used for God's purposes, it must be conquered and subjected to His will.

On this matter, Vegetius also said, "Few men are born brave. Many become so through training and force of discipline."[22] Similarly, few believers are born with tenacity and determination. The flesh never wants to endure hardship, get before the Lord in prayer, take on extra work, or deal with any difficult situation.

---

[21] Vegetius, *Concerning Military Manners,* I.xi.1.
[22] Vegetius, *Concerning Military Manners*, III.

Therefore, in order for the flesh to get in line and be used for God's purposes, it must be conquered and subjected to His will.

However, the flesh can be subdued only through constant, continuous "training drills" initiated by the Holy Spirit. Don't take lightly the practice exercises the Holy Spirit brings into your life. He is attempting to prepare you for a real battle!

BE SURE TO GO TO SWORD PRACTICE!

Because the Roman army was so committed to warfare, Roman soldiers *continually* practiced the arts of warfare. One primary, daily exercise was sword practice, which the soldiers engaged in both in the morning and the afternoon.

The Romans gave their recruits bucklers that were woven with willow branches and were *two times heavier* than the ones used in actual battle. In addition, the practice swords they used were made of heavy wood and were also *twice the weight* of the real swords they used in battle.

Every soldier practiced sword fighting by striking a six-foot-high wooden post that was firmly fixed in the ground. This post became the soldier's "enemy" during practice. Just as he would if he were fighting a real enemy, the soldier would advance on his target, strike hard with his sword, and then retreat.

The soldier's job in practice was to learn how to take advantage of his enemy and strike him at his weakest point in such a way that he could not respond. His aim was nearly always directed toward the area of the post that represented the head or face, the thighs and legs, or the sides of the torso.

Vegetius described Roman sword-fighting tactics in his book, saying, "They were likewise taught not to cut, but to thrust with their swords. For the Romans not only made jest of those who fought with the edge of that weapon, but always found them an easy conquest. A stroke with the edges, though, made with ever so much force, seldom kills, as the vital parts of the body are defended both by the bones and armor. On the contrary, a stab, though it penetrates but two inches, is generally fatal."[23]

The practices described above are exactly what Paul had in mind when he wrote, "...Take...the sword of the Spirit, which is the word of God" (Ephesians 6:17). How vital it is that we understand the sword of the Spirit!

Notice particularly where Paul said, "...the sword of the Spirit, which is *the word of God*." This word "word" is *not* the Greek word *logos*, which would refer to *the written word*. Instead, it is the word *rhema*, which refers to *a specific, quickened word*. This is a powerful distinction!

If Paul had used the word *logos*, meaning *written word*, it would have implied the sword of the Spirit deals a "sweeping stroke" against the enemy. However, this is not the case. In Scripture, *logos* refers to the Bible as a whole, and although the Bible is full of direction for our lives, it is not sufficient to give the enemy a fatal blow.

We need to *stab* the enemy! And in order to do that, we will need a *rhema* — a s*pecific, quickened word* from the Scriptures — placed into our hearts and our hands by the Holy Spirit. Once we have a *rhema* word from God, we have the "sword power" to render the enemy *powerless* in his attempts to steal, kill, and destroy everything good in our lives!

A genuine *rhema* does not have to be six pages long to be effective against the work of the devil. Remember, all a Roman soldier had to do in order to kill his enemies was to aim for a well-placed,

---

[23] Vegetius, Concerning *Military Manners*, I.xi.1.

two-inch-deep stab wound. Likewise, even one small *rhema* word from the Lord has enough power to *annihilate* the enemy. Thank God for the sword of the Spirit!

The best example of this powerful sword of the Spirit is found in Luke 4:3-13. In this passage, Satan repeatedly and aggressively attacked Jesus. But Jesus didn't respond by simply saying, "Satan, get out of here, or my Father is going to get you." Rather, Jesus "stabbed" him repeatedly with direct verbal blows! With each attack, Jesus countered with a specific quickened *rhema* from the Holy Spirit.

> **Once we have a *rhema* word from God, we have the "sword power" to render the enemy *powerless* in his attempts to steal, kill, and destroy everything good in our lives!**

After the devil tempted Jesus with food, Jesus drew the sword of the Spirit and rebuked Satan, saying, "...It is written, That man shall not live by bread alone, but by every word of God" (v. 4). The enemy had no response to the wisdom of Jesus' stab with a *rhema* word.

When Satan offered Jesus all the kingdoms of the world in exchange for worship, Jesus drew another *rhema* and wounded him deeply yet again. Jesus said, "...It is written, Thou shalt worship the Lord thy God, and him only shalt thou serve" (v. 8). To Jesus' anointed wielding of this sword of the Spirit, Satan again had no answer.

Finally, when Satan tempted Jesus to prove His deity, Jesus answered him again with a precisely aimed thrust of the sword of the Spirit. He said, "It is said, Thou shalt not tempt the Lord thy God" (v. 12). With this *rhema*, Jesus penetrated Satan's armor with one final stab and dealt his enemy a mortal blow.

When you are properly trained with the sword of the Spirit, you'll find that just as was true for Jesus, battles will cease to be a threat to your spiritual stability. Instead, they will become opportunities to prove your spiritual fitness!

Spiritual Armaments

Paul received his revelation concerning spiritual weaponry as he looked at the armor of the Roman soldiers throughout his ministry, and he used the analogy in his epistles more than once to describe our spiritual equipment. In Second Corinthians 10:4, he referenced this weaponry when he said, *"...The weapons of our warfare* are not carnal, but mighty through God...."* And the same is true in Ephesians 6:11 where Paul admonished us to "put on *the whole armour of God,* that ye may be able to stand against the wiles of the devil." This was an easy illustration for the apostle to use because he had been physically bound to many soldiers during his many imprisonments through the years.

Standing next to the imposing figures of these Roman soldiers, Paul could see their weaponry in detail, which consisted of:

- A loin belt

- A large breastplate

- Brutal shoes that were affixed with spikes

- A massive, body-length shield

- An intricate helmet

- A piercing sword

- A long, specially tooled lance that could be thrown from a distance to hit an enemy from afar

These pieces of weaponry were very, very heavy. Imagine how physically fit Roman soldiers had to be in order to carry such equipment!

Likewise, if you want to walk in the full armor of God and function effectively in the combat zone, you must be spiritually fit. Like the Roman soldiers of New Testament times, you must harden yourself through continual practice and obtain training in every possible maneuver against the enemy.

Where does your spiritual practice and training take place? *In your personal life and in the local church!*

When the enemy comes against you because you've taken a stand on the Word, it is time for you to fight. In fact, that attack may actually be an opportunity to practice for an even greater fight still to come. Never take an opportunity to "practice" spiritual warfare lightly!

Likewise, when your church leadership asks you for a greater commitment, they are giving you an opportunity to hone your spiritual skill set. They are trying to get you ready for the battles that lie ahead! Let them equip you, teach you, prepare you, and train you in every possible maneuver against the enemy.

> **When your church leadership asks you for a greater commitment, they are giving you an opportunity to hone your spiritual skill set. They are trying to get you ready for the battles that lie ahead!**

You must be in the constant practice of warring, fighting, destroying, and conquering in the spirit realm. It's your responsibility to fully and regularly immerse yourself in all the disciplines that accompany warfare and to undergo constant drills, military exercises, hardship, and training.

The following are examples of training exercises you can use to build up your spirit man and become better equipped for warfare:

- Attend services where the Word is taught and preached by the anointing of the Holy Spirit.

- Listen to teaching resources that will develop you spiritually.

- Daily engage in scriptural spiritual warfare.

- Regularly attend prayer meetings.

- Study and stand on the Word.

- Cultivate a deeper intimacy with the Lord in your prayer life.

- Sow into the Kingdom of God with your finances.

- Devote yourself more fully to doing your part in the work of the Lord.

Habitually engaging in these exercises will build in you a militaristic mindset. That mindset will then enable you to outlast your enemy in battle and emerge from the combat zone as the undisputed champion!

Returning to Second Timothy 2:4, we see that when Paul wrote, "No man that warreth…," he was conveying a wealth of information to his readers. He was likening our Christian commitment to the constant and necessary exercises, discipline, and drills of the Roman soldier.

This word "warreth" in the Greek is actually a present participle. This means the first part of Second Timothy 2:4 could be translated, *"No man warring, warring, and warring…"*; *"No man involved in constant combat…"*; or *"No man serving as a full-time soldier…."* Paul was stressing to us that as soldiers of Christ, our primary occupation is to be in the business of constantly engaging in full-time warfare against the enemy.

The Necessity of Carrying Burdens

Let's look now at what Vegetius wrote about the loads Roman soldiers had to carry. He said, "To accustom soldiers to carry burdens is also an essential part of discipline, recruits in particular should be obliged frequently to carry a weight of not less than 60 pounds (exclusive of their arms) and to march with it in the ranks."[24]

Vegetius then went on to explain why this kind of intensive physical training was so important: "This is because on difficult expeditions, they often find themselves under the necessity of carrying their provisions as well as their arms."[25]

We know that our flesh never likes to do anything difficult. However, there will be times when we must go the extra mile and bear the extra burden, and we must come to grips with this stark reality. Just as Roman soldiers were sometimes required to carry extra burdens in addition to their own food and weaponry, Galatians 6:2 teaches that we must "bear ye one another's burdens, and so fulfil the law of Christ."

By hardening ourselves through constant training and mental preparation, we can do *anything* that God requires of us. That is why Peter says in First Peter 1:13, "Wherefore gird up the loins of your mind...." We must keep our minds alert, prepared, and untangled from the fear of facing difficult situations.

---

[24] Vegetius, *Concerning Military Manners*, I.xviii.1.
[25] Ibid.

God's 'Boot Camp'

You must never withdraw from your divine assignment, even when the heat of the battle grows intense and the challenges seem overwhelming. That is why you should continually immerse yourself in the work of the local church, which is *God's spiritual boot camp*. There you learn how to endure hardness and subject your flesh to discipline. Your former titles, prestige, and worldly reputation cease to exist, and you are stripped of your civilian clothes. You have been enlisted by the Lord Himself and have become a soldier in His army.

> You must never withdraw from your divine assignment, even when the heat of the battle grows intense and the challenges seem overwhelming.

Once you are in God's army, it doesn't matter who you were in the world. What counts is your ability to forget your past and commit yourself completely to a new lifestyle of training and combat, so you can become the *fit* soldier that God intends you to be. In God's boot camp, you are a new soldier who needs to be trained, exercised, practiced, and disciplined until you are ready to fight.

To see yourself as a soldier in God's army doesn't remove His special attention from your life, and it doesn't make you less than special. On the contrary, the very fact that the Lord has enlisted you *makes* you special! He has handpicked you to join His army and fight at His side.

However, we must understand that being specially *selected* by the Lord is a very different thing than being specially *coddled*. In order for us to join the ranks of God's army in these last days, we must be willing to lay aside all of our past successes, worldly titles, and creature comforts and step out of our comfort zone. Then we must enter God's spiritual boot camp as new recruits to be trained, equipped, and sent forth. Every one of us is required to strip off our worldly garments, receive our number, and get in line to begin basic training. *Boot camp is for beginners.*

The constant discipline and the challenge to excel in the training of those enlisted in God's army may seem difficult for the moment. However, it's this kind of lifestyle that always makes spiritual girls and boys into great men and women of God — and that is a very good thing!

I've also heard people say things like, "The pastor should really use So-and-so more than he does right now. That person is a bank president." Or they might say, "What is wrong with the leadership of our church? God has just sent us a concert pianist, and they are not using him!" It's true that God has a place for these talented people, and in time, they will be used. But for the time being, they are *new recruits*. Before they can be used effectively in the local church, they must strip themselves of their former prestige and worldliness, get in line with the rest of the "recruits," and become disciplined through constant, rigorous exercise. Only then should they be used in the front lines of leadership. If this were our philosophy in the Church today, the Church would be full of committed, passionate, battle-fighting warriors instead of mere civilians with a "take-it-easy," "don't-make-it-too-hard" mentality.

> The constant discipline and the challenge to excel in the training of those enlisted in God's army may seem difficult for the moment. However, it's this kind of lifestyle that makes spiritual girls and boys into great men and women of God — that is a very good thing!

We must allow our officers to train us in every necessary maneuver! They are called by God to teach us how to march in rank, how to take every possible advantage of the enemy, and how to impact the world for Jesus Christ. And once they have helped us become battle-ready, they send us out into the combat zone to put our skills into practice.

> *The difficulty of the task does not change its necessity.* **God needs us to do what He has called us to do!**

Obeying God and doing the work of the ministry are not always easy endeavors. Sometimes in the midst of trying circumstances, God asks us to take on new responsibilities. In these moments, however, we have no choice except to buckle down, bear the extra load, and get the job done. *The difficulty of the task does not change its necessity.* God needs us to do what He has called us to do!

STAYING UNTANGLED FROM THE WORLD

Paul continued in Second Timothy 2:4 by saying, "No man that warreth entangleth himself with the affairs of this life…." This word "entangleth" is the Greek word *empleko*, which describes *a person entangled in his lower garments or caught in some type of vine.*

Perhaps the clearest example of the Greek word *empleko* ("entangleth") in the New Testament is found Matthew 27:29, where it is used to describe Jesus' crown of thorns. It reads, "And when they had *platted (empleko)* a crown of thorns, they put it upon his head…."

Think for a moment about how they made Jesus' crown of thorns: Jagged, thorny vines were carefully *woven together* until they formed a tight, crown-shaped ring. Taking this into account, we see that word *empleko*, describes *something that has been carefully woven together*. In fact, Matthew 27:29 could literally be translated, *"They had carefully woven together bunches of thorny vines into a crown...."*

By using this word *empleko* in Second Timothy 2:4, Paul was teaching that committed, warring believers don't enjoy the privileges of civilian life. Rewards will come to those who remain faithful, but they come only after the heat of the battle has passed. *The true spiritual warrior doesn't have time to be consumed with or distracted by the affairs of civilian life.*

A soldier who habitually thinks about life outside the combat zone doesn't change the war, but he does change his own effectiveness in the fight. Entertaining such thoughts serves only to turn a soldier into a lazy, uncommitted daydreamer who quits before his job is done and fruit is borne.

To truly live in the peace of God, you must be war-minded. As Vegetius said, "He, therefore, who desires peace should prepare for war."[26]

I encourage you to stop dwelling solely on your future and to start thinking about where you are at *right now*. It's wonderful to think about Heaven, and it's refreshing to think about relaxation and vacation. However, if bullets are flying all around you, you need to give those bullets your full attention! *You are in the midst of warfare.* Win your battle; *then* rest and relax.

Remember, you are living in the combat zone.

---

[26] Vegetius, *Concerning Military Manners.*

THE AFFAIRS OF THIS LIFE

You might be thinking, *What did Paul mean when he said that we shouldn't entangle ourselves with the "affairs of this life"? What exactly are we supposed to be untangled from?*

The key to this question is found in the phrase "affairs of this life" in verse 4. The word "affairs" is the Greek word *pragmeteia*, which refers to *a normal, regular daily regimen or preoccupation with civilian life*. In fact, we derive the word "pragmatic" from this Greek word, which refers *to the practical affairs of daily life*.

> It's refreshing to think about relaxation and vacation. However, if bullets are flying all around you, you need to give those bullets your full attention! *You are in the midst of warfare.* Win your battle; *then* rest and relax.

Thus, when this word is combined with the deeper layers of meaning we've already studied, a much fuller translation of Second Timothy 2:4 could read like this: *"No man who is serving as a full-time soldier, fighting on the front lines of battle and constantly warring, has the privilege of allowing himself to be woven together with the normal preoccupations of civilian life...."*

Why can't a soldier's thoughts and attention be woven together with the preoccupations of civilian life? Because he is a soldier — *not* a civilian. Soldiers should not be concerned with the same trivial matters that civilians are concerned with. Soldiers must keep their minds focused on warfare, or they may lose their lives!

Of course, there are basic affairs of life that we must diligently attend to, such as going to work, paying bills, etc. But we are not called to be so entwined in the busyness of everyday life that we get distracted from our assigned mission — taking territory for the Kingdom of God.

Soldiers grapple with the temptation to lose themselves in the daily affairs of civilian life. Regarding this, Vegetius wrote, "And if any long expedition is planned, they should be encamped as far as possible from the temptations of the city. By these precautions, their minds, as well as their bodies, will properly be prepared for service."[27]

Long-term warfare can make a soldier think longingly about a life far from the fray of battle. If a soldier is stationed in a camp that is close to a city, it's possible that the city lights, sounds, and aromas might tempt him to desert the battlefield and join the mainstream of civilian life. Soldiers had to maintain a constant militaristic mentality, and as such, they were not permitted even to *visit* a city. Civilian life was off-limits for them!

Likewise, we as Christian soldiers must draw the line between our pursuit of God and the fulfillment of our part in His plan and a preoccupation with civilian life. We cannot afford to sit idly by, thinking about how sweet it would be to experience the comforts of civilian life.

Daydreaming doesn't help you fight in the combat zone! You are a fighter, and you need to be concentrating on the job God gave you to do.

It is true that you can get in a wrong relationship with the affairs of this world that can tie your life in a knot, take your attention off the combat zone, and sidetrack you. In fact, when you abuse anything in life — whether it is money,

> We as Christian soldiers must draw the line between our pursuit of God and the fulfillment of our part in His plan and a preoccupation with civilian life.

---

[27] Vegetius, *Concerning Military Manners*, I.ii.2.

marriage, relationships, credit cards, or material goods — you are setting yourself in a downward spiral that, if not arrested, will lead only to future devastation.

Abuse, materialism, and neglect are all pitfalls that can open the door to the enemy in our lives and invite him into our camp. Of course, we have no choice but to deal with the practicalities of life, and there is nothing wrong with owning quality material goods or living in a comfortable house. But we must make sure that we don't allow ourselves to develop an unhealthy preoccupation with worldly possessions or responsibilities. We must keep them in our hands but not our hearts, so to speak.

However, Paul was *not* talking about material goods or possessions when he admonished Timothy to not become entangled in the "affairs of this life." As we discussed earlier, Timothy's life was being threatened, and his church was in decline. In the midst of these dire circumstances, he was tempted to become tightly bound up with a malignant, unseen substance that acted almost like a rope that was tied around him and secured with a messy knot.

What was this "rope" Timothy was in danger of becoming entangled with? *Self-preservation!*

RESIST THE GRIP OF FEAR!

Like the long tentacles of an octopus, it seems that a spirit of fear was reaching out to grab Timothy, hold him in bondage, and suck the life out of him. Had fear become a part of Timothy's normal, daily routine? Similar to a civilian who is preoccupied with the affairs of looming bills, car repairs, and so on, it seems Timothy was preoccupied with the possibilities of what "might" happen to him if he were arrested and possibly worried about trying to replace the church leaders who seemed to have deserted him in his hour of need. It appears that fear was Timothy's biggest problem in life.

Have you ever been gripped with fear? Perhaps it was a fear of failure or a fear of a lack of finances to meet a pressing need. Perhaps it was a fear of losing your friends or a fear that you wouldn't be successful in an important endeavor. No matter what your specific fear was, you felt those long tentacles reach out to grab you, hold you captive, and suck the life right out of you.

Just like Timothy, people sometimes allow fear to wrap itself around them and grab hold until they can't even function or think. In fact, sustained feelings of strong, overpowering fear can even lead a person to an eventual nervous breakdown! The absolute truth is that fear has the potential to completely destroy people if they don't deal with it quickly and decisively.

A spirit of fear can gain access and take hold through any open window in your life. A fear might seem small and insignificant at first, but that little fear, if left unchecked, will soon grow into a monster. It will keep expanding and expanding until you finally choose to do something about it.

For instance, suppose you have a fear of lack of finances. As you continually dwell on your finances day after day, you start to worry that a lack of money might hurt your ability to ever be successful. This leads you to develop a fear of failure. Over time, this fear grows and grows, getting stronger and more powerful with each passing day. Eventually, it becomes so strong that you begin to feel a small ache in your body. Now you start having a fear of sickness. This fear consumes you, and eventually your fear of sickness actually manifests as a reality in your body. *Fear will crush you if you let it!*

You may have great aspirations for your life — but if fear wraps itself around you, those aspirations are *on hold* until you conquer that fear.

There are times when fear has tried to grab hold of me. Like Timothy, I have lain in my bed in the middle of the night and cried out to the Lord to deliver me from fear (see Psalm 34:4). I had to deal with and overcome that fear just like everyone else.

Satan is the author of fear, and fear is a spiritual attack. Therefore, when fear tries to suffocate us and threaten our personal sanity, we must recognize it as an attack from Satan and *resist* it. We must command it to leave in Jesus' name!

> **When fear tries to suffocate us and threaten our personal sanity, we must recognize it as an attack from Satan and *resist* it. We must command it to leave in Jesus' Name!**

Over and over, the Bible warns us about fear because if fear grabs hold of us, we will not be able to please Jesus and complete the job the Lord gave us to do. When we walk in fear, we are like a walking time bomb, unstable and insecure and ready to explode at any minute.

We *must* make the decision to get rid of all forms of fear. *We are soldiers, and we don't have the luxury of accommodating fear in our lives.*

TAKE THE 'BIG LEAP'

One good scriptural example of a man overcoming fear is the story of Joshua. Joshua certainly had to deal with fear. He was a great, anointed leader, but he was also a man. How do you suppose Joshua felt when God said to him, "...Now therefore arise, go over this Jordan..." (Joshua 1:2).

What God told Joshua to do was an incredibly difficult thing to accomplish! At that time, it was flood season, and the Jordan River was flowing out of its banks. Yet God essentially said, *"Arise. Come on, I want you to take the big leap!* Just put your feet into the water. When you dip your feet into the water, the water will part for you, and you and your people will walk across on dry ground."

The easy part for Joshua was hearing God's command. *But that's always the easy part.* The real challenge is when you actually step out to do what God said! Putting your foot into the water is the hard thing to do — especially if you have already announced to everyone that the water is going to part!

As you prepare yourself to step out in faith, all you can think is, *What if the water doesn't part, and I look like a fool? What if it doesn't work?* Every leader and believer is faced with this same prospect at some point. Anytime God tells you to do something, you can be sure, fear will try to come and say, *'What if, what if, what if...'*

> We all have the opportunity at some point in our lives to become totally preoccupied with what *may* happen and then totally miss what God has in store for us to do.

We all have the opportunity at some point in our lives to become totally pre-occupied with what *may* happen and then totally miss what God has in store for us to do.

In light of all this, Paul essentially said in Second Timothy 2:4, *"No man who is serving as a full-time soldier, living in the combat zone, and constantly warring has the privilege of letting the nitty-gritty affairs of life get him down. A real combat-zone fighter has no time to be preoccupied with any affairs other than warfare...."*

A PERSONAL GOAL FOR EVERY SOLDIER

Paul continued his message to Timothy in verse 4 by saying, "No man that warreth entangleth himself with the affairs of this life; that he may *please* him who hath chosen him to be a soldier."

Particularly pay heed to the phrase, "that he may *please* him." Here Paul began to describe what every real combat-zone fighter should desire and aspire to in life. He said that the believer's goal should be that he may "…please him who hath chosen him to be a soldier."

The word "please" is the Greek word *aresko*, which always conveys the idea of something that is *virtuous, delightful, fit, perfect,* or *pleasing.* It was used in classical Greek literature to describe *horses that were trained, swift, beautifully proportioned, and a pleasure to watch perform.* These were superb horses.

By using this word, Paul was telling us what our chief desire in life should be. Although our spiritual training helps us win our personal battles, its primary purpose is to make us into the kind of Christians that God loves to watch in action! Our purpose should be to become so developed, fit, trained, and prepared that the Lord will enjoy watching us on the battlefield!

> **Would the Lord get pleasure watching the way you fight right now? Would He see you as one who is trained, prepared, and fit for service?**

Would the Lord get pleasure watching the way you fight right now? Would He see you as one who is trained, prepared, and fit for service?

We decide what God sees. It is up to us to determine what type of soldier we will be.

WHO IS YOUR ENLISTING OFFICER?

Notice the next phrase in verse 4, where Paul said, "…That he may please *him who hath chosen him to be a soldier."*

The phrase "who hath chosen him to be a soldier" is also very significant. This entire phrase is translated from the Greek word *stratologosanti,* which refers to the top-ranking officer who enlisted all the new recruits into the military.

Paul's use of this word tells us that Jesus Christ, our Enlisting Officer, carefully chose us to be in His army. He called us forth and conscripted us into His service, and He is now our *Commanding* Officer.

As Paul concluded Second Timothy 2:4, it is almost as though he said, "Your chief concern should be to make sure your Commanding Officer — the One who chose you, called you, and conscripted you into service — finds you well-trained and fit."

Our Commanding Officer will take full responsibility to care for us and to completely provide any provisions we might need. He will never let famine occur under His watch, nor will He allow disease to attack His ranks. Jesus will faithfully fulfill all of His duties as our Commanding Officer. Whatever we need in order to fight better, He will provide to us *freely.*

> In spite of His great care and provision, our Commanding Officer cannot force us to train, prepare, and become ready for the fight.

However, in spite of His great care and provision, our Commanding Officer cannot force us to train, prepare, and become ready for the fight. He can send equippers and trainers into our midst, but He can't make us obey them and submit to their authority.

That is why Paul concluded verse 4 by essentially telling Timothy, *"Timothy, the Lord is our Commanding Officer. He will provide everything you need to come out of this combat zone as the winner! However, you must make the decision to be a good soldier. He can't make this decision for you. Make it your aim in life to become trained, prepared, and fit to serve in the Lord's army. Make the Lord's personal satisfaction your highest aim. Remember: To please your Enlisting Officer is your most important business. Do whatever is required to accomplish this feat."*

A FINAL WORD ABOUT THE KING'S ARMY

In this chapter, we have seen what God expects from His army. We, the Church, must recognize that we are called to be more than pew-warmers, and *we must come to grips with the reality of warfare.*

It is time for us to move out of our comfort zone into the combat zone to which God has called us — to fight, to wage war, and to drive back the forces of hell!

Never again let us say that we are too tired, too weary, or too handicapped to obey our Commanding Officer. If we decide to fall in line, take our position, and march in an orderly fashion in obedience to His commands, He will provide everything we need.

In the next chapter, we will see how Paul switched from the illustration of a soldier to the illustration of an athlete. To compete in this game of life called "the combat zone," it is essential that you prepare and become fit!

Your competitor, the devil, is ready to take you on and pin you to the mat in defeat in the wrestling ring. He's ready to fight it out in a boxing match. Only a decision — *made by you and you alone* — to prepare for the fight will put you in a position to win this strategic fight for life.

CHAPTER SEVEN

TRAINING FOR THE COMBAT ZONE

*I*n Second Timothy 2:5, Paul switched from using militaristic language to utilizing a very different type of illustration. He wanted to convey some new concepts regarding commitment, determination, skill, and discipline — all of which are absolutely necessary to win a war in the combat zone. So the apostle introduced the illustration of a *professional athlete.*

Paul wrote in verse 5, "And if a man also strive for masteries, yet is he not crowned, except he strive lawfully." This word "strive" is from the Greek word *athlesis*, which described *a person who was involved in a tremendous athletic competition.*

At the time Paul penned this epistle to Timothy, there were both amateur and professional athletes, just like there are today. If a person was an amateur, he was not considered to be a very serious contender. However, if he was a professional, it was said that he was an athlete who was "striving for the mastery."

This kind of professional athlete aimed for the very top — *the mastery* — of his profession. He was determined to be the absolute best in his field. There was not an amateur bone in him; *he was totally committed.*

This kind of committed, full-time, professional athlete was exactly what Paul was referencing when he used the Greek word *athlesis* in his letter to Timothy.

Remember, in Second Timothy 2:3 and 4, Paul had already told Timothy to endure hardness as a good soldier of Jesus Christ and to be in the habit of preparing himself for combat. Timothy knew that in order to be victorious, he needed to become everything *in the Spirit* that a Roman soldier was *in the natural.* He needed to be:

- Fierce.

- Completely committed.

- Tougher than the adversary and hard at the appropriate times.

- Able to endure extreme climates, heavy burdens, and particularly long and tedious expeditions.

- Expertly trained in every possible maneuver against the enemy and with every available weapon.

Thus, when Paul shifted to the illustration of striving for the mastery as a professional athlete, he made a strong statement that confronted Timothy (and us) with a very important question.

COMPETE TO WIN!

Paul wanted Timothy to ask himself the following questions:

- *Am I serving the Lord just for fun? That is, am I an "amateur" who isn't really committed to going all the way? Am I just serving the Lord because it's popular, convenient, or fulfilling to do for the moment?*

- *Or am I a "professional" who is willing to pay any price, undergo any kind of preparation, work as hard as is needed, bear up under any pressure, and endure whatever is necessary until I come out on the other side as a champion of my appointed contest?*

We must constantly ask ourselves these same questions. It's fun to serve the Lord when there are no problems and it basically costs us nothing. We can go to church, give our tithes and offerings, attend meetings, pray and sing together, and so on — all at no great expense to our lives. However, if the situation changes and it suddenly costs us greatly to serve the Lord, our commitment is quickly put to the test.

For example, if problems emerge in your local church, how will you respond? Will you faithfully stand by and support your godly leadership? Or if the devil attacks your finances and makes it difficult for you to give, will you still serve the Lord by remaining obedient in paying tithes and giving offerings? *Are you an amateur, or are you a professional?*

Let's return to Paul's statement in Second Timothy 2:5: "And if a man also strive for masteries...." Particularly notice this word "man." It is the Greek word *tis*, which would be better translated as *anyone at all*. Paul's use of this Greek word *tis* tells us two important things.

> **Am I a "professional" who is willing to pay any price, undergo any kind of preparation, work as hard as is needed, bear up under any pressure, and endure whatever is necessary until I come out on the other side as a champion of my appointed contest?**

First, it reveals that *anyone* can register to compete in the fight of faith if he or she desires. Second, it tells us that anyone who decides to be a competitor had better understand the importance of undergoing the necessary preparation with proper training.

The mastery of an athletic skill is not attained without great effort. Yes, anyone can accept the challenge, but no one can win unless he goes through all the necessary steps. The rules are the same for each competitor. That is why Paul continued, "And if a man also strive for masteries, yet is he not crowned, except he strive *lawfully.*"

The word "lawfully" doesn't refer to the rules of the game, but rather to *the standard of training and preparation* that every professional athlete was required to complete before the game actually started. This is important because it tells us that we should never attempt to enter the arena of a God-ordained assignment until we have gone through the necessary preparation to win. *Winners are those who have faithfully trained and prepared themselves to win.*

THE HIGH PRIVILEGE
OF BEING A COMPETITOR

During New Testament times, there were athletic "scouts" just like there are today. Athletics were a big event to the Greeks, and the athletes who won the competitions were nearly adored and worshiped. Therefore, scouts would visit communities across the country in the hope of discovering new athletes. Their main goal was to find the most talented and fit young men to compete in the games.

When a scout found a prospective champion athlete, he would extend an invitation to him to attend a training camp. These young men were not forced to attend the camp, but many did because it was considered a high privilege in Greek society to be personally invited to become a professional athlete.

At camp, the new athletes were introduced to bodybuilders and trainers who were skilled in the arts of fighting and athletic competition. Then they were put on a rigid diet and exercise program. The trainers would put them through incredible workout routines in order to build both their bodies and their minds, because being *mentally alert* was deemed equally as important as being *physically fit.*

Timothy knew all about these matters. In fact, nearly everyone in First Century Greek and Roman societies knew about the strict, regimented training that athletes underwent in order to compete. It didn't require much thinking on Timothy's part to understand what Paul was inferring with the phrase "striving for the masteries."

However, can you imagine what Timothy must have been thinking to himself by this time? Just when he was about to catch on to Paul's instructions to be a *soldier,* the apostle Paul dramatically switched illustrations and in effect wrote to Timothy, *"Let me give you another example. Be like an athlete!"*

Paul's choices of illustrations in Second Timothy 2:3-5 are very important because they conveyed two very important points:

First, we need the commitment of a soldier because we are going to be out on the front lines. Sometimes our spiritual walk is going to be tough, but we have no choice in the matter. We are called to live and fight in the combat zone.

Second, we must commit to preparing like an athlete. Athletes don't just get up one day and decide to try fighting in the ring or running a marathon! They train and prepare constantly in the most difficult kind of way.

Many people think that once they're filled with the Holy Spirit, they don't need to use their minds or do any type of natural preparation that is normally required. However, this is a completely false assumption!

We must understand that we have been called by the Holy Spirit to train and prepare for what God has put us on this earth to do. *If we don't respond properly to the promptings of the Spirit, we won't be used.*

The Holy Spirit "scouted out" the world. He extended us a personal invitation to "training camp" through the message of the Gospel, and we responded. When we said *yes* to the Gospel, He brought us into the training camp — which is *the Church.*

In the Church, there are all kinds of "trainers" and "body-builders." They are called *apostles, prophets, evangelists, pastors,* and *teachers* (*see* Ephesians 4:11). These professional trainers in God's Kingdom are supernaturally gifted and equipped to help you develop your spiritual muscles and get you in good shape. God's appointed trainers know exactly how to put you on a correct and balanced diet of the Word, and they are skilled in motivating you to use your faith and exercise your spirit man. Your part is to *listen* to them and then to diligently *apply* what they say to your own life.

Leadership begins in the local church. Your part is to be faithful where God has planted you and allow Him to train you through the efforts of the local pastor and other ministry gifts. As you do, you will become equipped, prepared, and ready for any contest with the enemy that you face on the path ahead.

Strip Off Everything That Hinders Your Training

As we saw earlier, Paul used athletic language in verse 5 to illustrate how we should prepare, train, and equip ourselves in order to win the fight and receive the prize. However, this was not the first time Paul used athletic language to convey an important spiritual truth. In fact, similar references can be found throughout the New Testament. One powerful example is First Timothy 4:7, where Paul said, "But refuse profane and old wives' fables, and *exercise thyself* rather unto godliness." Let's take a moment to look at the word "exercise" in this verse because it provides tremendous insight into Paul's thinking.

This word "exercise" is the Greek word *gumnadzo*, which describes *an athlete who exercises naked*, which is the way most serious athletes often trained in New Testament times. To our modern minds, this statement might seem a little ridiculous. However, Timothy knew exactly what this word meant because he was from a Greek world.

In First Century Greek and Roman society, the word *gumnadzo* was used only to describe *hard-working professional athletes*. By using this Greek word, Paul conveyed a clear message to Timothy.

Timothy was facing very difficult times when Paul wrote his epistle to him. But instead of encouraging Timothy to sit back, take it easy, and relax, Paul admonished the younger minister to "exercise." Metaphorically, Paul was saying to Timothy, *"Strip off all your clothes, and get to work preparing for some serious competition!"*

There is another important nuance to the word *gumnadzo* that is crucial to understand in order to grasp the full meaning of Paul's statement in First Timothy 4:7. In early New Testament times, *gumnadzo* was frequently used to describe *athletes who were in training to participate in combat sports*. Specifically, it denoted the manner in which competitors prepared and trained to fight.

In the First Century Roman world, there were primarily three forms of combat sports — *boxing, wrestling,* and *pankration* — all of which were carried out in the nude.

It's very significant that Paul used a Greek word that was so connected to these combat sports. Thus far, every verse we've studied in this book has dealt with the vital character traits needed to survive in the combat zone — well-trained, skilled, disciplined, hard-working, and strong in endurance. Here in First Timothy 4:7, Paul continued to elaborate on these qualities, but in order to drive home a specific point, he began to utilize the almost barbaric analogy of the three most common combat sports of that time — *the boxer, the wrestler*, and *the pankratist.*

Let's pause for a moment to take an in-depth look at these three particular forms of combat sports.

SPORTS IN THE ANCIENT WORLD

First, the Greek and Roman boxers of the First Century were not like ours today. They were *extremely violent* — so violent that they were not permitted to box without wearing helmets. Without the protection of helmets, the boxers' heads could have easily been crushed during violent sparring of these early boxing rounds.

Of all the sports, the ancients viewed boxing as *the most* hazardous and deadly.

In fact, Roman boxers of that time were so brutal that they wore gloves *spiked with small metal studs*. At times the metal studs were *serrated* in order to make deep gashes in the skin of an opponent. And as time went on, boxers began using gloves that were heavier and much more damaging.

If you study the artwork from that era, it is quite usual to see boxers whose faces, ears, and noses were totally deformed because of these dangerous gloves. You will also frequently see paintings of boxers with blood pouring from their noses and with deep lacerations on their faces as a result of the metal studs on the gloves.

Believe it or not, even though this sport was so combative and violent, rules were very minimal. Clinching (holding the opponent's body to slow down a fight) was not allowed, "no clinching" was essentially the only rule to the game!

A Greek inscription from the First Century BC said of boxing: "A boxer's victory is obtained through blood." Truly this was a thoroughly violent sport.

Next, there were *wrestlers*. Wrestling was the most ancient of the combat sports. Because it was an essential part of the education of Roman boys in the wealthier classes, every adult male in those classes learned to wrestle. However, combat-sport wrestling was *very* different than simple wrestling.

Although not quite as ugly and bloody as the other two combat sports, combat wrestling was still very aggressive and dangerous. Certain rules applied to the competitions of this combat sport. For instance, some of the most violent fighting techniques weren't allowed in wrestling, such as blows, kicks, thrusts, throttle holds, twisting of the joints, and fighting on the ground. But although less injurious than the other combat sports, wrestling was still a bitter struggle to the end.

Then there were *pankratists*. Pankratists were a combination of the other two combat sports combined. The word "pankratist" is from two Greek roots, the words *pan* and *kratos*. *Pan* means *all*, and *kratos* is a word for *exhibited power*. The two words together describe *someone with massive amounts of power; power over all;* or *more power than anyone else*.

This, indeed, was the purpose of *pankration*. Its competitors were out to prove they could not be beaten and were tougher than anyone else! In order to prove this, they were permitted to kick, punch, bite, gouge, strike, break fingers, break legs, and do any other horrible thing you could imagine.

An early inscription says this about pankration: *"If you should hear that your son has died, believe it, but if you hear he has been defeated and retired, do not believe it."* Why? Because more died in this sport than surrendered or were defeated. Like the other combat sports, it was extremely violent.

THE 'HOUSE OF STRUGGLE' — WRESTLING WITH PRINCIPALITIES AND POWERS

Paul told Timothy in Second Timothy 2:5, "…If a man also strive for masteries, yet is he not crowned, except he strive *lawfully.*"

> We must undergo the necessary exercises, training, and preparation *before the battle begins*, because once it begins, our opponent *won't* abide by rules of fair play and there will be *no time* for preparation.

As we saw earlier, the word "lawfully" refers only to *the training and preparation before the fight.* By using this word "lawfully," Paul was exhorting us to prepare ourselves for the fight. We must undergo the necessary exercises, training, and preparation *before the battle begins*, because once it begins, our opponent *won't* abide by rules of fair play and there will be *no time* for preparation.

Spiritual warfare is intense! Therefore, you'd better prepare, train, and get ready for it *in advance.*

Paul also used the illustration of violent combat sports to talk about spiritual warfare in Ephesians 6:12. He said,

"For we wrestle not against flesh and blood, but against principalities, against powers, against the rulers of the darkness of this world, against spiritual wickedness in high places."

Take note of this word "wrestle." It is the old Greek word *pale*, which denoted *a bitter struggle* or *an intense conflict* and referred specifically to the three combat sports of ancient Greece and Rome. By using this word *pale*, Paul described our warfare with demonic forces as a fierce, bloody combat sport![28]

Similarly, when you are fighting demonic foes, there are few rules to the ways devilish forces attack. Therefore, you *must* be equipped, alert, and prepared before the fight begins. *Whoever fights the hardest, the meanest, the smartest, and the longest will be the winner of this "wrestling match" in the combat zone.*

There is another important nuance of meaning wrapped up in the Greek word *pale*. The athletes who competed in combat sports trained in a building called the Palaestra, the name of which was derived from the word *pale*. Because the word *pale* described *a bitter struggle* or *an intense conflict*, the name Palaestra actually meant *house of struggle*.

The Palaestra was essentially a palace of combat sports, dedicated entirely to the cultivation of athletic skills. Here could be found professional athletes of all kinds, including boxers, wrestlers, and pankratists.

All day long, the Palaestra was filled to overflowing with dedicated, skilled athletes "striving for the mastery" along with a myriad of different trainers, equippers, bodybuilders, and fighting experts. In addition, it was full of exercise equipment, weapons, and athletic equipment, weights, and so forth. Everything an athlete needed to prepare for a fight could be obtained inside the Palaestra if he would only take advantage of it.

---

[28] For an in-depth study on scriptural spiritual warfare, I recommend that you read my book, *Dressed To Kill.*

The Palaestra is also analogous to the Church! Just like the Palaestra, the Church is a huge and wonderful "palace" where Christians are being prepared to fight and compete like professional athletes. Everything the believer needs to prepare himself for the fight — Bible knowledge, training in character, gifts of the Spirit, patience, faith, and so on — is right there inside the Church. All a person must do is decide to take advantage of it.

Inside the Church, a believer can receive everything he or she needs in order to fight a good fight! *Everything*.

It's Time To 'Strip Off Your Clothes'

When a competitor or an athlete entered the Palaestra, he would first be taken into a room called the *apoduterion*, or *the undressing room*.

In this room, the athlete would strip naked. Although it was an undressing room, it wasn't a mere locker room. In actuality, it was *a preparation room*.

Often amateur athletes would venture into the Palaestra and read the daily docket in order to see who was competing that day. If the competition looked too fierce, many would simply turn away and return home. These were not truly committed athletes and fighters.

However, those who read the list and then stripped off all their garments were committed to fight! In fact, the very act of shedding one's garments was itself a statement. By undressing, the athlete was saying, "I am here, and I intend to endure to the end. I am going to go through the process of preparation because I'm going to fight with the intention of *winning!*"

In the middle of the *apoduterion*, or the undressing room, were huge, hot, steamy baths. In another section of the room were huge slabs of marble fashioned to resemble large tables. In this room, the athlete began his work of preparation by taking off his clothes and immersing himself in the steaming baths to cleanse his body. Once he was thoroughly cleansed, he would lie atop one of the marble tables — first on his stomach and then on his back — and his trainer would rub *a first application of oil* into his muscles and flesh.

Only after the athlete had undressed, bathed, and received the first application of oil was he ready to go into the next room. This next room was called the *aleiplerion*, and it was maintained at a perfect temperature for a *second* heavy application of oil.

Before we continue to look at the specifics of the armor worn by these athletes and fighters, let's examine how the *apoduterion*, or the undressing room, relates to our illustration of the Church as a "Palaestra." To do this, we must first consider the prerequisites of the *aleiperion*, the second room in the Palaestra where athletes received their second application of oil.

Athletes couldn't move into the *aleiperion* and receive their second heavy coat of oil until they had first bathed and received an initial application of oil in the *apoduterion*. In the same way, we cannot receive a heavy application of the Holy Spirit's anointing *until we have first adequately prepared ourselves.*

So how do we prepare ourselves to receive a heavy dose of the Holy Spirit's anointing? To answer this, we must examine the three activities of the undressing room: undressing, bathing, and receiving a preparatory application of oil.

> **We cannot receive a heavy application of the Holy Spirit's anointing *until we have first adequately prepared ourselves.***

The first thing an athlete did in the undressing room was strip off all of his dirty clothes. Let's see what the removal of clothes represents in the believer's life. Throughout the New Testament, the removal of sin, evil, and wrong attitudes is likened to the removal of old, soiled, and unwanted clothes. This reveals that sin and wrong attitudes should be dealt with just like old clothes: *They must be taken off, laid down, pushed aside, and put away forever.*

For example, in First Peter 2:1, Peter admonished believers, "Wherefore, *laying aside* all malice, and all guile, and hypocrisies, and envies, and all evil speakings." The phrase "laying aside" is from the Greek word *apotithimi*, which was used in a classical sense to denote *the removal of an old set of clothes*. By using the word *apotithimi*, Peter literally meant, *"Wherefore, remove these attitudes from your life as if they were an old set of unwanted clothes...."*

We see this Greek word *apotithimi* used in other verses as well. James 1:21 says, "Wherefore *lay apart* all filthiness and superfluity of naughtiness...." This phrase "lay apart" is *apotithimi*, which indicates James was saying, *"Wherefore, take off, lay down, and push away forever like an old set of clothes any and all filthiness and evil excess in your lives...."*

Likewise, Ephesians 4:22 says, "That ye *put off* concerning the former conversation the old man...." The phrase "put off" in this verse is also the Greek word *apotithimi*. Paul was teaching, *"Like an old set of clothes that needs to be taken off, pushed aside, and discarded, take off your old man and throw him away...."*

Finally, Colossians 3:9 says, "Lie not one to another, seeing that ye have *put off* the old man with his deeds." This phrase "put off" is also the Greek word *apotithimi*, which once again likens *the removal of sin and bad attitudes* to *the removal of one's clothes*.

The athlete of the Palaestra could not receive any application of oil until his clothes were first removed. Because the Palaestra represents the Church, it means that the true, committed contender — the believer who really wants to fight and win in the combat zone — must *first* make a decision to strip off the sin and bad attitudes and cast them out of his life. In fact, there can be no bathing, cleansing, and anointing until these "dirty, old clothes" are removed.

How could we possibly have a great anointing of the Holy Spirit in our lives if we carry wrong attitudes, anger, resentment, fear, and other such baggage around with us? If we truly want to be serious contenders in the combat zone, we must prepare ourselves. Laziness, slothfulness, hurt, anger, fear, resentment, animosity, and grudges — all of these must be stripped off us like an old set of clothes and discarded forever!

We must strip all bondages and excess weight from our lives. If we do not remove all of this undesirable baggage, we won't be in a position to receive our first or second application of the Holy Spirit's oil.

The oil belongs to those who strip off all hindrances and stand totally yielded, submitted, and naked before God.

Have you properly prepared yourself to receive this first application of the Holy Spirit's oil for your life?

> **The oil belongs to those who strip off all hindrances and stand totally yielded, submitted, and naked before God.**

DIP TO CLEANSE — THEN RECEIVE THE FIRST DOSE OF OIL

The second thing an athlete did in the undressing room was cleanse himself in the hot, steamy baths. This tells us something very important: After we've committed ourselves as genuine contenders in the fight of faith and stripped off our sin and bad attitudes, we must allow the blood of Jesus and the cleansing water of the Word to remove any residual sin that might still remain in our lives.

Like the athletes of old, we must dip into the hot, steamy, cleansing water to come up squeaky clean. *Our cleansing waters are the combined work of the blood and the Word* (*see* 1 John 1:7 and Ephesians 5:26).

Only after we've been thoroughly cleansed will we be ready for our first dose of oil — *but not until.*

After an athlete had stripped off all of his clothes and then bathed and cleansed himself, he was taken from the baths directly to the large, marble slabs. There he lay down on his stomach so his trainer could begin applying the first application of oil to his skin. However, no athlete could receive this first application until he was naked, bathed, and cleansed. *There were no shortcuts in this important procedure.*

This fact is also vital to our understanding of Paul's exhortation to Timothy in First Timothy 4:7. Remember, Paul admonished Timothy to *gumnadzo* ("exercise"), or *exercise while naked.* When Paul mentioned the word "exercise," Timothy surely thought of the three preparatory phases that an athlete underwent in the undressing room of the Palaestra. He and all of his contemporaries were well acquainted with the activities of committed athletes and the rigorous manner in which they trained and prepared for their competitions.

Likewise, before you receive your first vital application of oil, spiritually speaking, you must determine within yourself whether or not you are truly a serious contender.

- Are you going to be like those who find out the competition will be fierce and choose not to walk away?

- Are you willing to keep moving forward and never abandon the fight, even if the odds are against you?

- Are you willing to strip yourself of all that hinders you from preparing for victory in the combat zone — including wrong attitudes, laziness, slothfulness, unforgiveness, and fear?

- Are you willing to cleanse yourself — and then *keep* yourself cleansed — through the blood of Jesus and the washing of the water of the Word (*see* 1 John 1:9; Ephesians 5:26)?

- Are you willing to permanently turn away from the sin and filth of your past and leave behind the world and its ways?

All of these questions must be answered *yes* and then *acted upon* before the first application of the Holy Spirit's oil can be applied — the anointing and empowerment to do what God has called you to do. This is a necessary prerequisite to moving forward with God. And if you never receive the first dose of oil in your life, you'll never be taken "down the hall" to receive the second heavy application of the Holy Spirit's anointing.

> **Are you willing to keep moving forward and never abandon the fight, even if the odds are against you?**

Once an athlete had done all that was required to receive the first application of oil, his trainer would enter the undressing room carrying expensive rubbing oil and approach the large marble slab where the athlete was lying. The trainer would then begin to vigorously rub the oil into the athlete's skin — a task that could sometimes take hours.

As the trainer massaged the first application of oil into the athlete's skin, he would press harder and harder until the skin was soft, smooth, and supple and the muscles were toned and in good shape. This wasn't a normal body rub — it was a thorough work-over. The trainer's goal was to press the oil deeply into the skin, which made the rubdown *painful* at times.

By the end of this initial application of oil, all the pores of the athlete's skin would be saturated with oil so dirt and grime couldn't penetrate during the fight. The athlete had been made ready for his second, heavy-duty application of oil.

A Spiritual Picture

This first application of oil in the Palaestra paints a beautiful picture of our spiritual lives. We will receive this initial application of the Holy Spirit's anointing in our walk with God if we will:

- Strip off our sin and bad attitudes.

- Bathe in the cleansing blood of Jesus and the water of the Word in our everyday walk with Him.

- Enter the church with an open heart and completely submit ourselves to the work of a pastor in the local church.

- Allow our pastor to give us an ongoing, sometimes-chal-lenging work-over as he tones us with the Word.

After all of this vital work of preparation is done, we will be in a position to receive *the second application* of the Holy Spirit's oil in our lives that leads to a greater dimension of empowerment to do what we are called to do. However, if we are not willing to start with the necessary first steps, we will be restricted from receiving a greater anointing from the Holy Spirit.

It is the second application of the Holy Spirit's anointing that everyone seems to seek. But you must know this: *It is not possible to have the second until you have received the first.* This was not permitted for athletes in the Palaestra, and neither does God permit it in His Church. *There are no shortcuts in God.*

FIRST THINGS FIRST

In Second Corinthians 1:21, Paul wrote, "Now he which *stablisheth* us with you in Christ, and hath anointed us, is God." Notice the order of Paul's words in this verse. Before there is any mention of the anointing, Paul first talks about *being established.*

You see, we want to get things out of order sometimes. We want to dash right into the greatest anointing, the greatest power, and the greatest ministry. But it simply doesn't happen this way with God. He first requires that we become *established.*

By requiring that we become established before we receive His anointing, God isn't trying to hinder our progress. On the contrary, He is trying to *prepare us, train us,* and *establish us* in the Word.

The anointing of the Holy Spirit to enable and empower us to fulfill what He's called us to do is precious to God. So if we want to receive a greater anointing and handle it correctly, we must get first things first. First, we must become established.

You might ask, "But what exactly do you mean by 'established'?"

I'm talking about very basic ingredients of our spiritual walk, such as:

- Being dedicated to the Word

- Living a holy life

- Being submitted to a local pastor

- Becoming a faithful tither

- Faithfulness in service to the local church

- Church membership

If these basic qualities are absent from your life, there is no way you can be ready for a greater anointing of the Holy Spirit.

In Second Corinthians 1:21, the word "stablisheth" in Greek is the word *bebaios*, which literally means *to make firm, steadfast, or settled*. It describes something that is *immovable and set in stone*.

Paul's intention in this verse is clear. He was saying, *"If you want to be used in the greater anointing of God, develop these firm, steadfast, immovable, and settled traits in your life. Become established!"*

> God will not use us until we decide to become qualified to be used. We must inwardly resolve: *I'm here for the fight! I'm yielding to the Holy Spirit's work in my life as He helps me strip off every bad attitude, every bad habit — EVERY weight that hinders me from moving forward in God.*

God will not use us until we decide to become qualified to be used. We must inwardly resolve: *I'm here for the fight! I'm yielding to the Holy Spirit's work in my life as He helps me strip off every bad attitude, every bad habit — EVERY weight that hinders me from moving forward in God.* If we make this decision, we put ourselves in a position to receive the anointing of the Holy Spirit.

After Paul talked about being established in Second Corinthians 1:21, he continued by saying, "Now he which stablished us with you in Christ, *and hath anointed us*, is God."

So we see that the first step in your spiritual walk is to establish yourself in the local church, submit to a local pastor, and allow him to press the Word and the first application of the Holy Spirit's oil deep into your life. Then God will take you to the next phase of your spiritual experience — the greater anointing!

Please understand, your commitment to the local church, like an athlete's commitment to the Palaestra, is not an option. It is an absolute requirement! Your sustained dedication and commitment to serve within your church family where God has planted you will cause the Holy Spirit to issue you an invitation to enter into the second anointing chamber. There you will receive the second, heavy-duty application of the Holy Spirit's oil for your life.

OILED FROM HEAD TO TOE
WITH A SECOND DOSE

Once the athlete had been effectively coated with his first layer of oil, he was taken into a second room, known as the *aleiplerion*. In this room, he was given a second, even more lavish application of oil.

The trainer would take a large vial of oil, turn it upside down, and completely pour it out over the athlete until his body was completely covered. This was a *thick* coat of oil that would remain on the athlete's body until the competition was over. In fact, references in early Greek literature tell us that these athletes looked like they had literally been greased. It was almost as if someone took a great crock of cooking oil and rubbed it all over the athlete's body from head to toe.

You may ask, "Why would they pour this oil all over the athletes?" For one thing, this second, heavy application of oil made the athlete *slippery*. Therefore, when he entered into the fight, his adversary would have difficulty grabbing hold of him.

There is something else you need to know about this rubbing oil. Although there was a huge storage room full of oil in the Palaestra, the oil was not free. The head official of the Palaestra — known in ancient times as the *gymnasiarch* — had to pay for it out of his own pocket.[29]

The anointing was free to the athlete, but it was extremely expensive to the one in charge of his training.

THE HIGH VALUE AND PERFECT TIMING OF THE HOLY SPIRIT'S OIL

> Christians sit in church and freely receive of the Word and the anointing, often unaware of the great price that the ministers put forth to obtain it.

The Church, like the *Palaestra*, contains a great storage of oil. In fact, all the oil of the Spirit we'll ever need is stored away in the Church. Just as the athletes of ancient Greece were anointed in the *aleiplerion*, Christians sit in church and freely receive of the Word and the anointing, often unaware of the great price that the ministers put forth to obtain it.

You see, although the anointing is free for believers who are training to do the work of the Lord, this precious anointing is not free to those who are applying it. In a very real way, those who minister have paid for this anointing "out of their own pockets" by their personal consecration to the Lord and to their call. Of course, the oil of the Holy Spirit isn't obtained with cash or credit cards; the Lord gracefully

[29] Michael B. Poliakoff, *Combat Sports in the Ancient World* (New Haven, CT: Yale University Press, 1987), p. 14.

imparts it to those who have demonstrated dedication, commitment, seriousness, sobriety, holiness, and hard work.

In addition, because the oil used in the Palaestra was so expensive, the head trainer, or *gymnasiarch*, was often unable to afford all the oil necessary to anoint the athletes. When that was the case, he would invite other trainers to help him purchase the anointing oil.[30]

This is an amazing picture of the ministry of spiritual leaders. The pastor is a wonderful gift, but the pastor alone cannot provide all the oil of the Holy Spirit you need. The same is true for evangelists and teachers. Similarly, the apostle is powerful and absolutely vital to your spiritual growth, but he is just one person and thus cannot provide all the oil necessary either. And although prophets might minister with a miraculous anointing and great utterance from the throne of God, they cannot provide all the oil needed.

There is no way one person can provide all the oil that is needed. It simply isn't possible. Therefore, God brings together a multitude of professional "oil-rubbers" and suppliers who are anointed by the Spirit in their own lives and have received Heaven's call to help freely apply it to the spiritual athletes of the Church.

One other important point I want to emphasize about the second application of oil: It wasn't doled out randomly or in just any room of the Palaestra. It was applied in an *aleiplerion*, a special anointing chamber that was *temperature-controlled*. The heavy anointing was withheld until the temperature was correct; only then was the oil applied.

This indicates that there is a perfect temperature and atmosphere — a perfect place and time in our lives — for the heavy anointing of God's Spirit to come upon us. If we want to receive that extra measure of the Holy Spirit's anointing, we have to

---

[30] Ibid.

follow His leading in our lives so we will be in *the right place at the right time* to receive it.

THE REAL EXERCISE BEGINS

Once this second heavy dose of oil had been applied to the athlete's body, the real exercises and hardcore preparation began.

The athletes were taken into a small room, similar in shape to a modern cubicle. It was a small room with no roof, and sand covered its floor. This training room was designed to catch the heat of the sun, turning it into a kind of sunbox or hotbox.

> If we want to receive that extra measure of the Holy Spirit's anointing, we have to follow His leading in our lives so we will be in *the right place at the right time* to receive it.

We are told by some historians that the temperatures in this room rose so high that an average man who had never endured such heat would have *died* if he was left there too long. It was in rooms like this that the athletes trained, fought, and prepared for their real fights.

You may be thinking, *Why in the world would athletes practice in such sweltering heat?* Because the real competitions always took place during the hottest period of the year. And although many were skilled and athletically fit through all kinds of grueling exercises, they were not able to endure the intense heat of the sun. With all of their skill and training behind them, at times athletes still failed and were defeated *because the heat wore them out.*

Likewise, that is often the problem with believers who have only a head knowledge of the Word. They study books, listen to audio and video teachings, and receive what other men have to say, but their knowledge is only skin deep. When they get out in the heat of the conflict, they find out that they haven't truly absorbed the Word into their hearts, and, as a result, they're unprepared for the heat of the battle.

We need to be ready to take some heat — and we must never be afraid of the heat! Yes, it's uncomfortable, and sometimes it's nearly unbearable. However, we are called to step out into the intense heat and say, "I'm going to learn to take it, fight in it, and *win* in the midst of it!" As we do, we will rise to join the ranks of combat-zone fighters of the highest caliber!

THE HOTTER THE CONFLICT, THE SLIPPERIER THE OIL

Keep in mind that Greek athletes were covered with a thick layer of oil! Although this intense heat in a small, open-ceiling room was difficult to endure, it actually worked to the athlete's advantage. The hotter the conflict was, the slipperier the oil became on his skin!

In the context of this illustration, this fact says something wonderful about the Holy Spirit. When the devil turns up the heat in your life to the point where the conflict seems unbearable, that heat actually makes you more yielding to the anointing of the Spirit. And if His anointing is allowed to flow freely in the midst of a heated battle, it won't matter how hard Satan tries to seize you — you'll just slip

> We are called to step out into the intense heat and say, "I'm going to learn to take it, fight in it, and *win* in the midst of it!" As we do, we will rise to join the ranks of combat-zone fighters of the highest caliber!

right out of his hands! You'll suddenly become a target that he can't catch!

How would you like to be so anointed that the devil could never catch or keep you immobilized in the grip of an attack? *Thank God for that heavy dose of the Holy Spirit's oil.* However, *you* can catch and immobilize the devil! Here's why.

When the slippery, oiled-up athletes of the early Greek world fought in the hotbox, they would smack their hands down into the sand floor. Because their hands were already covered with oil, sand would stick to their palms and make them gritty like sandpaper.

This sand served a very important purpose: It provided much-needed friction to the athletes' grip, which greatly improved their grappling abilities. Although their opponent could not hold on to them, they had no problem grabbing and holding on their opponent! That oil, mixed with the sand, gave them the ability to hold on to the enemy tightly, giving them *the edge* against their competitors!

Likewise, the Holy Spirit's anointing in your life always gives you the edge over the works of Satan. As you do your part to prepare for the contest and trust in the Lord to do *His* part, you will always have the upper hand!

EXERCISE WAS BEGUN
TO THE MELODY OF A FLUTE

In the Greek Palaestra, every athlete did the same exercises. For instance, besides practicing wrestling, wrestlers also practiced boxing. Conversely, boxers also wrestled in addition to performing their boxing regimens. Every athlete working out and training in the Palaestra attempted to become fit in each of the three combat sports: boxing, wrestling, and pankration.

Perfection was every athlete's ultimate goal. In fact, athletes were so committed to perfecting their skills, they viewed athletic competitions as a beautiful art form. In fact, they even sought to incorporate *rhythm* into their movements. Pay careful attention to this: Long-jumpers, discus throwers, boxers, wrestlers, and pankratists practiced and competed to the accompaniment of the flute!

Can you imagine what it would be like to throw the discus to the tune of a flute? Or how about boxing to the accompaniment of the flute? Can you envision those pankratists kicking, biting, hitting, striking, breaking fingers, snapping backs, and so on — *all to the accompaniment of a flute*?

These athletes were so committed to moving their bodies with rhythm and beauty that when they competed, they allowed their movements and motions to be dictated by the volume and tempo of the flute! If the flute played faster, they moved faster; if it played slower, they moved slower. If it played louder, they fought more forcefully, and if the music grew soft, they were more low-key in their attacks.

Do you see how this metaphor applies to our lives spiritually? We need to be so fit, exercised, and spiritually prepared that we can fight and compete in the combat zone to the accompaniment of the Holy Spirit!

Whatever sounds the Holy Spirit is making, *that's* the sound we need to follow.

> Whatever sounds the Holy Spirit is making, *that's* the sound we need to follow. We need to be fine-tuned to flow *precisely* to the accompaniment or "melody" of the Holy Spirit.

When He tones it down, we need to tone it down. When He increases the volume, we need to increase our attacks against the adversary. We need to be fine-tuned to flow *precisely* to the accompaniment or "melody" of the Holy Spirit.

STRONGER AND TOUGHER

Furthermore, Greek athletes did everything they could think of to become tougher. They exercised with weights and punching bags; they did calisthenics; and they engaged in shadow-boxing, kicking, gouging, etc. They did whatever it took to prepare for future contests. They wanted to become stronger and tougher!

The athletes followed a very rigorous regimen that included a day of preparatory exercises, a day of intensive workout, a day of rest, and a day of medium-intensity exercises. This regimen applied to every athlete, regardless of his physical condition. Even if an athlete was sick, this was his schedule to sustain.[31]

These athletes were fully committed to becoming hardened. They wanted to be able to take *anything* their opponent dished out. Therefore, they made their daily lives difficult so that when they were confronted by a real challenge, they could easily overcome it.

Greek athletes were so committed to winning that if they became wounded, they refused to allow their opponent to know it. An early example of this fierce determination is a story of an ancient boxer. He was hit extremely hard by his adversary right in the middle of his mouth. In fact, the blow was so hard that it knocked out many of his teeth! But rather than opening his mouth to spit out the broken teeth and blood, which would have alerted his opponent to his stricken condition and thus added more fuel to the fire, *he chose to swallow his teeth!*

---

[31] Poliakoff, p. 17.

I think this is a wonderful example of how believers are to wage warfare in the combat zone. When they become wimpy and sit around constantly complaining, they are actually encouraging the devil to hit them again.

It's like a boxer who just stands in front of his opponent with his hands at his side, unwilling to defend himself from the next punch. In the same way, a person is handing out an unwitting invitation to the enemy by continually saying things like, "My feelings are hurt!"; "Oh, the devil's out to get me!"; or, "I'm so wounded by what that person did."

It's one thing to ask others to pray for you to be mended and healed. But it's another thing entirely to sit around moaning and groaning because you've been hit by one of Satan's attacks! Why let the devil know that he dealt you a hurtful blow? That's what *faith* is for! Rise up by faith, stand on the Word, grab hold of the Holy Spirit's powerful anointing, and go after the devil for another round! Keep fighting till you've obtained the victory that Christ won for you in His death, burial, and resurrection!

There is a place in God where you must decide to *keep moving forward*, regardless of what has happened or what *will* happen. You must come to the place where you say, "I don't care how bad my feelings are hurt. I don't care how many times I've been stomped on. I'm *not* going to give the devil the satisfaction of knowing I've been wounded! I'm going to get back up and *fight*!" This is the place of fierce, immovable determination you

> Why let the devil know that he dealt you a hurtful blow? That's what *faith* is for! Rise up by faith, stand on the Word, grab hold of the Holy Spirit's powerful anointing, and go after the devil for another round!

must come to if you are going to qualify as a genuinely serious combat-zone fighter.

If believers developed this type of mindset, there would be a lot less *flesh* in the Church and a great deal more *victory*. As it is, local churches are frequently populated with people who have never taken off their old clothes and positioned themselves in a place of preparation. Yes, they come to church and listen to the message. But many of them have never really made a decision to enter into the first room to strip, cleanse themselves, and be "worked over" by the Lord and His anointing.

> **Every one of us has to make the decision to strip off all of our sin and bad attitudes, come into the "Palaestra" — the training ground of the Holy Spirit — and let Him prepare us to *fight*.**

Instead, the Church today seems to be crowded with people who only want spiritual shortcuts. Many believers have convinced themselves that they are somehow exempt from all the preparation, exercise, training, and hard work needed to succeed in the combat zone.

But that is self-deception. Every one of us has to make the decision to strip off all of our sin and bad attitudes, come into the "Palaestra" — the training ground of the Holy Spirit — and let Him prepare us to *fight*.

A DIVINE AND *GENEROUS* CONTRIBUTION OF NEEDED SUPPLY

We've talked about that special measure of anointing that comes when the need arises to fulfill God's purposes in a certain situation. But it's important to note what Paul wrote in Philippians

1:19 that pertains to the Holy Spirit's anointing in our lives. Paul wrote, "For I know that this shall turn to my salvation through your prayer, and *the supply of the Spirit of Jesus Christ.*"

Especially notice that last phrase, "...the supply of the Spirit of Jesus Christ." The word "supply" in this verse is extremely significant to the issue of the Holy Spirit's anointing because it reveals just how much anointing is available to us at *any given moment* in our daily lives that we need His supernatural supply.

This word "supply" comes from the very old Greek word *epichoregias.* What an odd word this is! Literally translated, it means *on behalf of the choir.*

You may ask, "What does a choir have to do with the anointing of the Holy Spirit, and why does Paul use such an odd word to describe the Spirit's provision in our lives?" The answer to these questions is found in the wonderful history of this word *epichoregias.* It involves the story of an ancient choir that nearly went broke.

The story took place in ancient Greece. After many months of preparation and training, a renowned choir and theatrical performance ran out of money just when it was about time to stage a large musical presentation for the public. The actors and musicians had been training for months on end, but it looked as if all their hard work and dedication was in vain. For all intents and purposes, running out of money meant their show was over, and all their labor, tears, work, and commitment would amount to nothing.

However, a very wealthy citizen from the area heard about the plight of this choir. Because the people had worked so hard, he couldn't stand the thought of all their labor being wasted. Therefore, he came to them and gave a financial contribution "for the choir."

This contribution was so massive, it overwhelmed the choir members. In fact, it was far too much money! They didn't need this vast sum, and they didn't know what to do with it all. It was an incredible contribution made "for the choir."

This Greek word *epichoregias* ("supply") comes from that story. By using this word, Paul was plainly telling us, *"When you have done all you can do — when you've trained, worked, prepared, and done your part — then God comes in to make a contribution on your behalf! He gives you an enormous "supply" of the Spirit. There is so much of the Holy Spirit's anointing available to you that you'll never know how to use it all. If you tried to exhaust that divine supply, you would find it was impossible. God has made a supernatural, exceedingly abundant contribution of the Spirit's anointing into your life!"*

Do Heavenly Prizes Await Us?

Going back to Second Timothy 2:5, Paul was telling Timothy to get ready for a fight. He wrote, "And if a man also strive for masteries, yet is he not crowned, except he strive lawfully." By using athletic terms, Paul made his message clear and simple. He was telling this younger minister to stop feeling sorry for himself and letting the devil know he had hit him hard. In essence, Paul was saying, *"Get up and do all you can to prepare and train to fight this fight. You've still got a job to do and a devil to overcome!"*

So far, we've covered the phrases "strive for masteries" and "strive lawfully." However, there is one extremely important part of this verse we have yet to examine — the phrase "yet is he not crowned."

This word "crowned" is significant because it conveys yet another vivid image to Timothy (and to us)! The Greek word for "crowned" is the work *stephanos*, which denotes *a diadem, a royal crown*, or *a crown of glory*. There is no room for wondering what Paul's statement about this crown implies!

Paul continued with the illustration of athletic events, but by using the word *stephanos* ("crown"), he moved beyond the rules, preparation, and training and began to talk about *the rewards that were given to the best athletes*. Those who finished first in the games received a beautiful crown made out of laurel leaves. It was this crown that Paul was explicitly referring to.

When you understand the connotations carried with this crown — *this reward* — you will know why the athletes were willing to pay such a high price to compete.

I pray to God that we, too, would understand the magnificent rewards that Jesus Christ has waiting for us! In Revelation 22:12, the Lord Jesus says, "And, behold, I come quickly; and *my reward is with me....*"

Paul never lost sight of his reward for service. Remember, he said, "Henceforth there is laid up for me a *crown of righteousness*, which the Lord, the righteous judge, shall give me at that day..." (2 Timothy 4:8).

Likewise, in Second Corinthians 5:10, Paul wrote, "For we must all appear before the judgment seat of Christ; that every one *may receive* the things done in his body, according to that he hath done, whether it be good or bad."

Often we become so involved in the training, preparation, and heat of the conflict that the conflict is all we can see. We can become so involved with our current conflict and fight of faith that we cease to see *beyond* the fight to the reward that is awaiting us because we were faithful to the end! Or we become so consumed with the conflict that it is all we can see or think about, and we forget that Jesus Christ is waiting and has *His reward* in

His hand. *Unfortunately, when we slip into this state of mind, we have become nearsighted and forgetful.*

THE CROWN OF VICTORY

This "crown of glory," "diadem," or "victor's crown" was reserved for the winner of a competition. In Second Timothy 2:5, Paul used it to describe what God has waiting for those dedicated believers who fight a good fight of faith.

If you won an athletic victory in classical Greece, the ancients placed a laurel crown upon your head. The crown was merely crafted out of laurel leaves and nuts, sometimes apples or pinecones, and twine, so it wasn't worth much in and of itself. However, it carried a far greater kind of worth because it represented something very important. It was symbolic of a promise.

> We can become so involved with our current conflict and fight of faith that we cease to see *beyond* the fight to the reward that is awaiting us because we were faithful to the end!

In today's world, we might simply give the winner a large check representing a huge cash gift — but in those days, there were no checkbooks. Therefore, during the huge ceremonial celebration after the contests, the crowd gathered to watch the victor receive his award. Then the victor would be given a crown, which represented *monetary rewards*.

Not only was money given the victor, but other material possessions were occasionally awarded as well, such as homes, servants, and other luxuries. These rewards were so great that the entire ancient world knew about them. This, of course, explains why athletes were willing to undergo such adverse training and discipline. It wasn't just for the sake of discipline and endurance — they wanted that huge material reward!

There's still more! In addition to all the material rewards, the greatest winners were often nearly deified. Monuments, statues, and huge memorials were built to commemorate their victories. Many of these statues still stand to this very day — living memorials of their accomplishments.

What Does All This Mean to You?

Like Timothy, you probably have had to deal with some type of adversity in your life. In fact, you may be dealing with a struggle *right now.* Would you like to see your situation changed? Would you like to see this continuing conflict end?

If so, Second Timothy 2:5 is just for you! Paul admonished us, "And if a man also strive for masteries, yet is he not crowned, except he strive lawfully."

If you determine to go after your prize like a professional and if you're willing to strip the extra baggage from your life, you'll see your circumstances turn around. You'll end up the winner — and you'll receive the victor's crown!

Like the professional athletes of old, determine to take a difficult stand — even in the midst of adverse circumstances. As you steadfastly continue to stand in faith, no matter what comes against you, your fight will be remembered in the ages to come!

Think of all the great men and women of God from the past whom we still remember, read about, and attempt to imitate. Their strong stance of faith and their fierce determination to win the fight has forever placed them in our hearts to be remembered.

Because they fought so well, we remember people like Paul, Timothy, Luke, and John, as well as many giants of the faith who have lived in recent centuries. All of these godly men and women are remembered today — not for their education or worldly titles, but rather for their unwavering dedication and accomplishments by faith!

Hebrews 11:32-39 says:

> **And what shall I more say? for the time would fail me to tell of Gedeon, [Gideon] and of Barak, and of Samson, and of Jephthae; of David also, and Samuel, and of the prophets: Who through faith subdued kingdoms, wrought righteousness, obtained promises, stopped the mouths of lions, quenched the violence of fire, escaped the edge of the sword, out of weakness were made strong, waxed valiant in fight, turned to flight the armies of the aliens.**
>
> **Women received their dead raised to life again: and others were tortured, not accepting deliverance; that they might obtain a better resurrection: And others had trial of cruel mockings and scourgings, yea, moreover of bonds and imprisonment: They were stoned, they were sawn asunder, were tempted, were slain with the sword: they wandered about in sheepskins and goatskins; being destitute, afflicted, tormented; (Of whom the world was not worthy:) they wandered in deserts, and in mountains, and in dens and caves of the earth. And these all, having obtained a good report through faith....**

These faithful ones are with us in our minds *forever* because they "obtained a good report through faith." In the same way, God has called you to "endure hardness as a good soldier of Jesus

Christ." He has also called you to "strive for masteries" to the end that you will be rewarded both now and in the life to come!

Your strong, consistent, determined faith will put you on the map!

This was the message Timothy needed to be reminded of — and you need to be reminded of it too!

CHAPTER EIGHT

REAPING THE BENEFITS
OF THE COMBAT ZONE

*I*n Second Timothy 2:3 and 4, we saw that Paul used the picture of a Roman soldier to instruct Timothy on how to approach spiritual warfare. Verse 5 then changed course as Paul abruptly changed the illustration to a professional athlete striving to be the very best in his field.

Then Paul switched illustrations once again to make another very important point about how we should view our life in the combat zone. In verse 6, the strenuous athletic talk abruptly stopped, and Paul used the picture of a hard-working farmer.

Paul had already told Timothy to endure and fight like a *soldier* and to prepare and train like an *athlete*. Now Paul was telling Timothy to work hard like a *farmer*.

It was almost as though Paul said, *"Timothy, you need to be a good soldier of Jesus Christ! But as good as that analogy is, it isn't complete. You also need to train and prepare like an athlete does. You must also develop the determination and commitment of an athlete. And finally, I want to add one more: You need to be hard-working like a farmer! Really, Timothy, you need to develop all three of these traits. You must fight like a soldier, train like an athlete, and be committed to work hard like a farmer. You must view yourself as a soldier, an athlete, and a farmer!"*

A HARD-WORKING FARMER

In Second Timothy 2:6, Paul wrote, "The husbandman that laboureth must be first partaker of the fruits."

In this verse, there are four very important messages. Take note of the words "husbandman" and "laboureth" and the phrases "must be" and "first partaker of the fruits." By using these words and phrases, Paul was conveying very specific pictures of farm life. As you read on, you will see how these four pictures relate to those of us who are living in the combat zone.

First, Paul mentioned the "husbandman." The word "husbandman" is the Greek word *georgos*, and it refers to *one who tills or works the soil*. It would also be accurate to translate *georgos* as *a soil-worker* or *a soil-tiller*. This was a common Greek word with a very definite meaning, so there is no doubt that Paul was referring to the activities of *a hard-working farmer*.

Furthermore, notice how Paul continued: "the husbandman *that laboureth...."* The word "laboureth" in Greek is the word *kopos*. The word *kopos* doesn't refer to regular work, but rather *to the hardest type of work*. Today one might say this was a man investing his "blood, sweat, and tears" in his work.

By using the word *kopos*, Paul was painting a picture of a farmer working in the heat of the afternoon sun during the hottest season of the year. The ground is hard; there is little moisture; and the work is *strenuous*.

The farmer is plowing and sowing. After he finishes working one row of his garden, he turns at the end of the row and starts plowing and sowing all over again on the next row. By the end of the day, this farmer is physically exhausted, mentally drained, drenched with perspiration, and covered with dirt. He has done a hard day's work!

By using this illustration, Paul was telling us that living in the combat zone can be difficult and exhausting. However, rather than complain and moan about it, we may as well face the fact that someone has to get out there and do the job! And if we don't do the job where our own lives are concerned, the work will go undone and no harvest will be reaped.

> If a farmer wants to reap the benefits of a crop, he has to plow and plant, regardless of the difficulties he must face to get the job done. The unbearable heat doesn't change the necessity of the task.

If a farmer wants to reap the benefits of a crop, he has to plow and plant, regardless of the difficulties he must face to get the job done. The unbearable heat doesn't change the necessity of the task.

If we faithfully do our job in the combat zone like a hard-working farmer, we will reap the benefits of our harvest. As Paul said, "The husbandman that laboureth must be first partaker of the fruits" (v. 6). The fruits belong first to the hard worker. Everyone else eats after him!

FARMING IN THE MIDDLE EAST

The tradition of farming in the Middle East reaches back for thousands of years, and the farming activities of the First Century AD are well documented. Documentation indicates that at least 50 Greek authors contributed written material on the subject of farming, but the majority of these actual writings have been lost forever.

Fortunately, many records written by Roman authors from the same time period have survived to this day. On the subject of farming, for example, three ancient Roman writers stand out for their detailed accounts of agricultural practices. Varro, a wonderful scholar, farmer, politician, and soldier who lived in the century preceding the birth of the Jesus, wrote tremendous details about the life of a farmer. Columella was another prominent First Century agricultural writer who recorded many details about farming in that period. And, finally, the famous Roman statesman and author, Pliny the Elder, wrote a large body of material, a substantial portion of which was dedicated to the study of country life, farming, and husbandry.

History reveals that in the countries where Christianity flourished, a highly organized system of farming had been set in place over the centuries. For instance, the areas surrounding Israel were established agricultural areas. It was for this reason that Jesus often used farming examples in His parables. These were examples taken directly from the lifestyle that affected the majority of the people during His time.

In fact, most scholars agree that until recent years, the historic methods of farming used in Israel and the surrounding Mediterranean areas had changed very little from thousands of years ago. This means that the same methods of plowing, sowing, and harvesting that were in use during the time of Jesus were still in use until quite recently. Therefore, it is easy for us to obtain an accurate picture of what Paul meant when he compared us with a hard-working Middle Eastern farmer of the First Century.

THE TASK OF SOWING SEED

The farming techniques for sowing and reaping that Paul referred to were not performed with highly developed machinery. Rather, they were nearly all done *individually by hand*. This is an important point when we consider that Jesus likens the teaching and preaching of the Word to the work of a farmer.

In Matthew 13, Jesus related two parables in which He used the illustration of a *farmer* (or "sower") to describe the preaching of the Word. In both parables, the farmer is *personally involved* in the sowing of seed and the reaping of the fruit.

Jesus likened the teaching and preaching of the Word to sowing the seed of God's Word into a man's or a woman's heart. Jesus said, "...Behold, a *sower* went forth to sow; and when *he sowed*..." (Matthew 13:3,4). Jesus used this same language again in verse 24, saying, "...The kingdom of heaven is likened unto a *man* which sowed good seed in *his* field."

Notice that in both of these examples, the sower himself went into the field to sow the seed. Also, notice the personal, individual touch in Jesus' words. He didn't say "many sowers went forth"; he said "*a sower.*" This statement is in perfect agreement with the historic records we have of the farming methods used during that time period.

The farmer was *personally involved* in all the activities of the field. It was *his* farm; therefore, it was *his* responsibility. His farm was so precious to him that it required his complete, total attention.

There is another important point to be found here: *Sowing the seed in the field was accomplished primarily by one individual.* Even though it was very time-consuming for one person to do all the work of sowing the seed, it was still the farmer's responsibility to sow and no one else's. Later when harvest time came, many workers could come into the field to help reap the harvest. However, the planting of seed — because it was such a crucial job — was the task of the farmer himself.

You may ask, "Why is this important?" Because it tells us that we must become *personally involved* in the work God has called us

> Each of us has been given a trust over God's "field" — the part of His harvest that He has made *us* responsible for as we fulfill what He has called us to do. We cannot depend on someone else to do our job for us.

to do. Each of us has been given a trust over God's "field" — the part of His harvest that He has made *us* responsible for as we fulfill what He has called us to do. We cannot depend on someone else to do our job for us. Neither can we simply bring in "hired hands" to help because we are exhausted or tired of our assignment. Fulfilling our ministry to people by extending God's love and sowing His Word in their hearts is important, and we must give that responsibility — in whatever arena of life we are called to — our own personal touch.

Maintaining a Personal Touch

We live in a day when Christianity has in many ways become computerized, highly mechanical, and mass-produced. Thank God for all of these technological advances. Because of them, the Gospel is being spread to every corner of the world. We use many of these methods in our own ministry; however, we must never forget that the Gospel needs a personal touch. It's so easy to reach people through television, radio, satellite, the Internet, the mail, and so on, that some people have come to neglect the warm, caring, personal ministry that should *always* accompany the Gospel.

For the most part, the new, modern ways of reaching people for the Kingdom of God are easy and non-threatening, which makes it easier for believers to engage nonbelievers. Anyone who has ever participated in door-to-door evangelism knows the feeling a person gets when a door is slammed in his face for attempting to share the Gospel. It is far easier to simply put out a mass email. If people don't like what a believer has to say, they can just delete the message.

Please don't misunderstand me. I'm thrilled for the countless numbers of people who are being reached via these different methods. I'm thrilled with *any* method that brings people to Jesus Christ, and I believe we must learn how to use every improvement in technology that exists. However, we must never allow these advanced methods to replace the personal touch of "the sower." First and foremost, sowing should be done *by hand*.

There is still no replacement for:

- The caring, personal touch of a *pastor*.

- The powerful, personal influence of an *apostle*.

- The penetrating, personally impacting message of a *prophet*.

- The fine-tuned, personal delivery of a *teacher*.

- The fiery, personal presence of an *evangelist*.

- The warm-hearted, personal impact of a *believer* on a lost or hurting soul!

It's true that electronic methods of reaching people are becoming commonplace and more acceptable as society evolves into an electronic world. But if using electronic means to reach people is all we do, we are missing a vital element — *the human touch.* Although our ministries might grow and our outreaches expand, we who are sowers of the Word into the lives of others must make every effort to be personally involved with the field.

HOW DOES THIS APPLY TO THE COMBAT ZONE?

When warfare is all around you and the battle is getting more heated, it would be easy to back up, protect yourself, and let someone or something else do all the work for you.

> **When rejection has hit you over and over on many different occasions, the temptation for you might be to withdraw. But this is Satan's strategy to keep you out of the field! He wants to keep you and the anointing of God on your life away from the saints.**

When rejection has hit you over and over on many different occasions, the temptation for you might be to withdraw. But this is Satan's strategy to keep you out of the field! He wants to keep you and the anointing of God on your life away from the saints.

There is nothing more powerful than the anointing being passed to others through our lives. Regardless of the spiritual climate or the difficulty of the hour, we must be directly, personally involved when it comes to planting the Gospel seed into the hearts of men.

Like a diligent farmer who works his field — plowing through hardened soil and sweltering heat during the hottest time of the year — we cannot neglect our responsibility to sow. Even if the task is difficult, we must do it. If we don't give it our all, the job will not get done properly before God. Therefore, our place is to be is in the field.

TWO PRIMARY METHODS OF SOWING SEED

There were two primary methods used to sow seed in Jesus' time. With the first method, the ground was *prepared* — *plowed* and *made ready* — to receive the seed. Once the ground was properly prepared, the seed was scattered and then sown into the ground by the farmer.

The second method used a different approach. Instead of first tilling the ground, the seed was scattered over hard, unprepared soil. Later it was plowed under as the farmer worked it over with his plow and oxen.

Of the two methods, the first worked better. This first method is also a good picture of sowing the Word *inside* the Church. Within the Church, we have the opportunity to work the soil, prepare the believers' hearts, and get them ready to receive God's Word. Then after the seed of the Word is sown, it can be worked further and deeper into the people's hearts by constant teaching.

Another factor of that first method of sowing in Bible times is that the farmer would walk along the straight, furrowed rows of soil that he had carefully prepared beforehand carrying a bag of seed. As he walked, he'd scatter the seed with controlled, sweeping motions left and right so that the seed landed on the good soil.

This picture of sowing seed into prepared soil forms an excellent picture of ministry. It is representative of sowing God's Word into the prepared hearts of a church congregation. The church is always good soil in that the majority of hearts of those attending church are there because they *desire* to hear the Word and the Holy Spirit lives inside them.

However, there are two ways to do this in a church congregation. A preacher can scatter the seed randomly, or he can maximize the effectiveness of the seed by strategically aiming it to land in the orderly, furrowed rows he has prepared.

Careful sowing into furrowed rows is better than simply scattering the seed randomly on the soil. It also helps the reaper when it comes time to harvest the fruit of the field. *The more orderly the planting of the field, the easier the reaping of the harvest of lines that are matured in Christ and bearing fruits of righteousness, holiness, and blessing.*

Preaching the Word to a congregation or a large crowd of people can be like scattering seed randomly on good soil. It is effective to an extent, but it is a challenge to preach or teach to the entire group in a way that will produce fruit in the lives of all who are present. In fact, the bigger a field is, the greater the challenge to make sure that seed is sown into the entire field in a way that will produce the intended harvest.

> **Armed with the Holy Spirit's wisdom and anointing, a minister can deliver a message that lands in hearts already prepared to produce the desired harvest.**

Why is this the case? In any one group, a multiplicity of problems and backgrounds are always represented. Therefore, it isn't always possible to zero in on a specific need. One message must encompass the range of issues faced by those present — negative mental strongholds, marriage difficulties, physical challenges, problems in finances, other personal problems, etc.

This requires every pastor to sow strategically from the truths of God's Word as he or she is led and anointed by the Holy Spirit to "scatter" the seed. The Spirit of God knows the needs that are present, and He will help the one who is ministering maximize the effectiveness of the seed that is being sown. Armed with the Holy Spirit's wisdom and anointing, a minister can deliver a message that lands in hearts already prepared to produce the desired harvest.

However, there is another way to plant the seed of God's Word that exponentially increases the lasting effectiveness and the size of the ultimate harvest. It entails planting the seed by hand into the carefully prepared ground of individuals' hearts in a deliberate, orderly fashion. That is what *discipleship* is all about: personally planting the seed, covering it with protection, watering it, and pouring fertilizer on it in order to ensure its growth.

There is another important point to take into consideration. When a ministry gift sows the Word from the pulpit, the minister should endeavor to bring order to his message, even though he is attempting to scatter the seed into the hearts of as many people as possible during that service.

A message from God that is organized, flows seamlessly from a previous message, and links with a series of messages is often helpful in keeping the rows of plants (the people!) on track and in order. On the other hand, disjointed messages can be confusing to the saints. People need help to keep their spiritual lives in order. Many of them do not have the capacity to organize their thoughts on how to implement the commands found in God's Word. They actually desire order and organization. Therefore, it is the preacher's responsibility to help them!

> The more strategic and orderly the sowing process is from beginning to end, the easier the harvest.

To reiterate — *the more strategic and orderly the sowing process is from beginning to end, the easier the harvest.* Ministry leaders must make the process as effective as possible in order to help the saints grow to their fullest extent and bear fruit that remains for God's Kingdom.

SOWING ON HARDENED SOIL

The other method of sowing I mentioned earlier (scattering seed upon hardened soil) is representative of sowing seed *outside* the Church in the world. It symbolizes preaching to the lost and sending the Word into a spiritually desolate society that is unprepared to receive the seed because hearts are not right with God. Furthermore, once the seed has been sown, the soil must be deeply plowed over and over again, or the seed will not take root. This process is made especially difficult because the spiritual soil is hardened.

When I think of those believers who have given their lives to reach pagan countries or who are endeavoring to reach large, spiritually barren cities, I can't help but think of a farmer working on hardened soil. We must pray for those called to work these difficult fields where the soil is totally unprepared to receive spiritual seed and there is little sensitivity to the things of God. *This is the most difficult method of sowing spiritual seed.*

> We must pray for those called to work these difficult fields where the soil is totally unprepared to receive spiritual seed and there is little sensitivity to the things of God. *This is the most difficult method of sowing spiritual seed.*

In addition to symbolizing the evangelistic ministry, this second method also represents sowing spiritual seed into a backslidden church. When a church family is spiritually complacent, backslidden, and "stuck in neutral," it can be quite difficult to sow seed into their hearts.

Thank God for pastors who have helped prepare the hearts of their people. A congregation with prepared hearts is a joy to teach! They soak up every word they hear! On the other hand, preaching to a congregation that has no appreciation for the Word and no desire to hear more of God is an extremely difficult challenge. In such cases, a minister must ignore the congregation's lack of response and continue preaching with all his heart. He must resolve to *dig* and *plow* until he penetrates the hardened ground and plants that seed deep down on the inside of their hearts.

This type of ministry is not fun!

However, whether it is enjoyable or not, *it must be done.* That is why God calls Timothy (and us) a "husbandman," or *a farmer.* Our job is *to get that seed into the field.* This is why Paul calls us the "husbandman that *laboureth....*" That means there are times when the work of sowing seed is truly a laborious task!

Keep Your Eye on the Weather, Bugs, and Birds

The time of year that a farmer chose to sow his seed was also very important. The newly planted seed could be easily affected by weather, bugs, and birds. Jesus referred to these devouring birds in the parable of the sower and the seed in Matthew 13. He called them the "fowls of the air," and they represented *demonic devourers* sent forth to gobble the Word out of the human heart.

The serious, responsible farmer was always careful to watch as the young crops grew and matured. It is noted in ancient texts that in the Mediterranean regions, the early spring winds could be vicious. This type of weather, of course, was a danger to the soil and seed as well. A strong windstorm could turn the soil, thus carrying away the precious seed.

It is therefore interesting to note th*at the most violent weather of the year always coincided with the perfect time to plant seed.* This is often true in the spirit realm as well.

When the time is right and God provides a brand-new open door in your life to reach people, strong winds will likely start blowing. Winds of opposition almost always accompany the planting of the Word into the soil of others' hearts — as well as the receiving of the seed into the soil of our own hearts.

However, we must not be afraid of the vicious winds of opposition. Neither can we wait until the winds have ceased to plant our seed. If we wait, we will undoubtedly lose our opportunity for harvest. Therefore, no matter what winds are blowing, we must seize the opportunity, get out into the field of our God-ordained purpose, pray over our seed, and plant it in the ground of people's hearts. We *cannot* allow the winds to dictate our obedience!

> **No matter what winds are blowing, we must seize the opportunity, get out into the field of our God-ordained purpose, pray over our seed, and plant it in the ground of people's hearts. We *cannot* allow the winds to dictate our obedience!**

Furthermore, because new crops faced so many threats, a good farmer would stay close to the field throughout the growing period to ensure its safety — especially while the crop was still young and immature. If foul weather, including hailstorms, and birds, locusts, or other insects attacked, his job was to be in that field doing everything within his power to protect the tender plants from destruction.

Likewise, it is the sower's task to protect the work of God with all diligence. One who sows God's Word must keep his eye on the crop, which is God's growing, maturing Church. This is especially true when the plants are young and are just beginning to take root. This is when the enemy will attempt to attack, destroy, and devour the seed of God's Word that was so recently planted in people's hearts.

At the time Paul penned his second epistle to Timothy, the younger minister was realizing that his own field, the local church in Ephesus, was under attack. After several years of good growth, an unbelievable demonic storm had arisen with a vengeance against the Early Church.

A wave of persecution against believers of Jesus Christ was creating the worst catastrophe in the history of the young Church. Many believers were being blown about by the vicious winds of fear, and many others were being swept away by death itself.

However, Timothy could not retreat like others had done to wait for the storm to blow over. His task was to be in the field. The fact that this satanic opposition was coming against him was the greatest indicator that he was *in the right place at the right time* to plant seed in the combat zone and to guard it so that a harvest could be reaped!

WINDS OF OPPOSITION TODAY

Although we don't have to deal with an evil emperor like Nero today, we do have winds of opposition and demonically induced foul weather attempting to buffet the Church on many levels. Strange teachings, doctrinal error, seducing spirits, rebellion, betrayal, and sabotage are all vicious winds that have the power to disturb the soil of a new believer's heart and carry away the seed that was planted within him or her. In the same manner, a young church — or even a longstanding church that has recently experienced a new vitalization by God's Spirit — can be adversely affected by the various winds of satanic attack.

For example, Satan has been successful at times in orchestrating disappointing situations in which some spiritual leaders have been discredited in the eyes of some people. The fallout from these situations can be catastrophic for some people, causing them to be offended and even ruining their trust in godly leadership. When that happens, Satan's strong, vicious winds succeed in carrying away precious seed as they destroy the faith of a number of new or spiritually immature believers.

Many churches and ministries today are experiencing "foul weather" in the area of finances. The winds of opposition try to drive the sowers out of God's harvest fields. What a demonic strategy that is! *Drive the sower out of the field so his harvest will never come in.*

But if we allow those opposing winds to dictate to us, we will be driven back into self-preservation, defensiveness, and defeat. We can rationalize to ourselves and say, "Maybe we should sit back and wait awhile," but that would simply delay the harvest. And should we ultimately fail to do what God has asked us to do, there will *never* be a harvest. Therefore, we must defy the odds, take authority over the foul weather generated by the kingdom of darkness, and *get back into the field.*

Your situation will *not* get better later if you do nothing but try to hunker down and weather the storm. As soon as you start planting seed again, the winds will return. Therefore, you must learn to do what God has called you to do, even if it looks like you may have to sow your seed in the face of a spiritual *tornado*!

The truth is, the very fact that the winds are blowing strong often means you are doing your job right and at the correct moment. *Foul weather nearly always accompanies the planting of seed.*

SOAKING THE SEED WITH PROTECTION

By the time of the New Testament, chemicals had already been introduced into agricultural practices in order to protect seeds from insects. As primitive as these chemicals were, they worked.

In the First Century, before any seed was sown, they were first soaked in a powerful liquid solution. This solution didn't hurt the seed, but it was deadly to the vile insects that would attempt to eat the seed once it was placed in the soil.

Soaking the seed was crucial!

Similarly, we must cover the seed of God's Word with prayer and the blood of Jesus Christ. If we thoroughly saturate our preaching and teaching with prayer — *before we speak the Word* — far less spiritual seed will be devoured by the enemy.

Often we become so busy preparing to sow the Word that we neglect the vital task of saturating the seed with prayer. Yet our prayers act as *protection* for the seed as it takes root in the ground of people's hearts. If Satan cannot blow the seed away, he will attempt to send in his *"creepy crawlers"* to burrow in and devour the seed right in the soil. But if the Word we speak forth is covered and soaked in prayer, those "creepy crawlers" — bad attitudes, inward or hidden sin, demonic attacks, doubts or accusing thoughts that the enemy inserts in people's minds, etc. — will be repelled. This is the only way we will see a more secure spiritual

> **Often we become so busy preparing to sow the Word that we neglect the vital task of saturating the seed with prayer. Yet our prayers act as *protection* for the seed as it takes root in the ground of people's hearts.**

rooting and a greater harvest of fruitfulness take place in God's people.

The "insects" that come to devour the seed show up in many forms. But the important thing for us to remember is that we must soak the seed in the first place with the vital protection that prayer affords so that it *can't* be eaten!

HAS THE ENEMY ATTACKED YOUR PERSONAL FIELD?

Has this been a description of you? Has your life, business, church, or ministry been attacked by demonic "fowls and insects"? The infestation may have originated from the wrong attitudes or misdeeds of other people. Or perhaps it was an outgrowth of your own unrenewed soul. Regardless, this type of "creepy crawler" effect can leave you sowing, sowing, and sowing with no results.

> **Every farmer occasionally experiences a crop failure. But a farmer doesn't stop farming just because of one bad year! He has too much invested in his farm to give up that easily.**

I have met many people who testify that Satan's work of infestation began before they realized what was happening, and in the end, it resulted in some type of failure. Satan attempts to attack covertly, so this occurrence happens occasionally with any person who is trying to cultivate a dream into reality. If this describes you — if Satan found a covert inroad to infiltrate your church, ministry, business, or dream — you must remember that God has plenty of new seasons planned for your life and they're still ahead of you!

Like it or not, every farmer occasionally experiences a crop failure. But a farmer doesn't stop farming just because of one bad year! He has too much invested in his farm to give up that easily. He has put years of work into that farm, invested lots of money into his machinery, and has given his life to his profession. And he knows that just because one crop failed, it doesn't mean the next one will fail as well!

Likewise, you have too much invested in your church, ministry, business, or dream to give up now. You may have put years of work into it and planted all your finances in it. And you have invested in too much "spiritual machinery" to stop planting now. Just because one crop failed *doesn't* mean you're finished. When God speaks to your heart and you know it's time to start planting again, go for it!

Fear may try to keep you from trying again. However, you must think of yourself like that farmer. He doesn't stop farming because he's had one or even several bad years of farming. He keeps planting that seed in anticipation of a bumper crop because one good bumper crop can make up for all those bad years of failure!

So pick up your bag of seed and start planting the Word in people's lives — and in your own heart — once again. If you recognize that you made mistakes in the past, make any necessary changes in order to be a better farmer the next time around.

Soak that precious seed in prayer and the blood of Jesus before you plant the next crop. Protect it, watch over it, and wait patiently for your crop to come in. *Your next spiritual season may be that bumper-crop year!*

Harvest Time Finally Arrives

The Bible has much to say on the subject of harvest. Psalm 126:5 says, "They that sow in tears shall reap in joy." Ecclesiastes 3:2 (*NLT*) says there is "...a time to plant, and a time to harvest."

Eventually, the time to reap the benefits arrives for every hard-working farmer.

Take note of this important fact: The time of harvesting in Bible days depended entirely on the *temperature, altitude*, and *climate* in each farmer's specific area of the nation.

Even today in Israel, altitudes and temperatures vary tremendously, so harvest comes at different times of the year for different areas. In one low-lying district, for example, harvest may be in full swing while in other districts at higher altitudes, harvest may still be weeks away.

Temperature, altitude, and *climate* determine the harvest time for each area. Rarely do all areas simultaneously harvest. But this is good news! If every area had to be harvested at the same time, there wouldn't be enough workers to bring the harvest from all the fields into the barn! It would put a strain on the entire community, and much of the harvest would be left to rot in the fields and be wasted.

Because harvest time varies from area to area, it permits the workers to work one area after another. This also gives the laborers space to rest a little between harvests, and it gives them time to develop in the art of reaping. In fact, these varied harvest times are responsible for producing the finest reapers. These reapers experience such great opportunities to practice their skill, and as a result, almost none of the harvest is lost.

SHOULD WE BE JEALOUS OF ANOTHER'S SUCCESS?

Can you recall a moment when you experienced feelings of jealousy over the success of someone that you would consider a peer or colleague?

For instance, often pastors and even church members feel left out, hurt, or upset when they hear of a neighboring church that is experiencing more growth than they are. The same can be true for businessmen and women who feel that they come up short when they measure the growth of their business to other comparable businesses in their region.

Perhaps you're in the ministry, and you've been working hard at pursuing your call for a long time with pure motives, yet you still haven't experienced much success. When that's the case, it may be confusing for you to deal with another minister's success, especially if you've observed a lack of faithfulness and integrity in that person's life. It can almost make you look at yourself and ask, *What's wrong with the way I'm steering this ministry? Why are we not experiencing that kind of growth? Lord, am I doing what I'm supposed to be doing? Am I out of Your perfect will?*

There is nothing wrong with asking those kinds of questions, but you should never *assume* that you're doing something wrong. It's always good to look inward and examine yourself. If you are in some way hindering the way God wants to move or if you need to make changes in your personal life or style of ministry that will speed up His harvest, it's vital for you to be aware of that fact.

So take the time periodically to examine yourself and assess the state of your church, ministry, or business — or whatever dream God has given you that you're pursuing. But as you do, you must not forget that the harvest depends on these three things in particular — *temperature*, *climate*, and *altitude*.

Perhaps you live in a city where the "temperature" isn't right yet for a large harvest. Perhaps the spiritual climate is still being prepared for a move of God's Spirit. Or it may simply be that your colleagues reached harvest time a little earlier than you did. However, none of these scenarios are proof that you have missed out on anything. All they tell you is that your climate is not ready just yet to yield a harvest. *Nevertheless, harvest time will come.*

You can see how the change of climate directly affects harvest time when you look at the way God touches nations, states, or even cities. For a while, a major move of God will consolidate in one area of a nation. Then the move of God will seem to subside in that area as His Spirit begins to manifest His power in another area whose harvest time has come. Then after the new field has been transformed and a great harvest brought in, God may move the emphasis of His reaping once again.

Does the fact that God shifts His focus for harvest to a new location mean that He is finished with the previous area or that He is simply leaving out some vicinities altogether? No! *Each region will come into a period of reaping and harvesting according to its own temperature, climate, and altitude.*

This principle applies to your church, ministry, business — to *whatever* your God-given assignment is. If the seed has been sowed and nurtured, guarded, and protected, every aspect of your labor for the Lord will come to fruition according to His perfect timing! Soon enough the climate will be just right for you to reap an incredible harvest.

> If the seed has been sowed and nurtured, guarded, and protected, every aspect of your labor for the Lord will come to fruition according to His perfect timing!

Who Does the Reaping?

Although the farmer was personally responsible to sow the seed into the soil, it was *impossible* for him to bring in the harvest on his own. Therefore, many workers were employed to help him with the task of reaping.

When the harvest was just beginning to come in, the farmer and his immediate family did the reaping. This early harvest was small and easy to handle with just a few people. The farmer's family took great joy in reaping the firstfruits; after all, this was what they had been working so hard for all along! Doing the initial reaping was their way of enjoying the firstfruits and of inspecting the new harvest to see how bountiful it was.

If it looked like it was going to be a bumper-crop year, the smart farmer had trained and prepared workers "on call" whom he could call upon for additional help. When the farmer and his family could no longer handle the harvest on their own, he would send word to these trained reapers, who would then come and assist him in the joy of reaping.

Once again, this analogy paints a wonderful picture of the local church. A pastor can handle a small, early harvest on his own and pick the firstfruits, but it isn't possible for him to handle a massive harvest without help. Therefore, like a smart farmer, a pastor must prepare the saints, equipping them to do the work of the ministry (*see* Ephesians 4:12).

If willing believers are trained and equipped before the harvest comes, then reaping and harvesting will be a joy! However, if God sends a large harvest and there are no trained workers to bring in the crops, that huge harvest can become a *curse*. Instead of the sower seeing the full potential of his labor realized, most of the harvest from that seed will be wasted, left to lie rotting in the field.

Unfortunately, this has happened over and over again in the Kingdom of God. Many large, God-sent harvests have rotted in the fields solely because of a lack of preparation. Many churches spend years praying for a large spiritual bumper crop. But when it finally arrives, they miss their opportunity because they didn't train and make the preparations needed to bring the harvest into the barn. I can't count how many times I've heard churches say, "We just didn't realize so many people would respond! We weren't ready for this kind of response. We simply were not prepared."

What a shame it would be to finally experience the move of God in your church, ministry, business, or community — and then to miss your opportunity to reap the harvest because you weren't prepared.

Let's be careful not to make this mistake. We must do our vital work of preparation before harvest time arrives!

How To Get Rid of Locusts

Another significant danger a farmer faced was the threat of his crops being devoured by *swarms of locusts*. Locusts were one of a farmer's primary causes for concern and fear. To a family whose sustenance depended almost entirely on the success of their crops, these bugs were the worst possible nightmare. Just one large swarm of locusts could ravage an entire field in a matter of days — *sometimes in a matter of hours*.

> **What a shame it would be to finally experience the move of God in your church, ministry, business, or community — and then to miss your opportunity to reap the harvest because you weren't prepared.**

To make matters worse, farmers living in the days of the early New Testament didn't have pesticides to remove these horrible scavengers from the plants in their fields. And because the locusts were so numerous, it was *impossible* to remove them by hand. There weren't enough workers in the entire land to combat the clouds of countless locusts that could light upon one man's field. Besides that, locusts eat so fast that any field would be totally destroyed before the work to eradicate them had even begun.

Locusts also didn't make their grand appearance until the crop was grown and it was time for harvest. Why? Because they wanted something to chew on! Prior to harvest time, there was nothing of consequence for the locusts to devour. So these destructive insects waited until the seed had grown and the beautiful crop was nearly matured and just about ready to be reaped. *Then* they would come and eat up everything in their path.

The locusts came to devour the fields at harvest time!

For many hundreds of years, it seemed there was no remedy for this situation. If a farmer's field was infested with locusts, he simply lost his harvest. However, at some point farmers made a discovery that allowed them to devise a counterattack against this incessant scourge of those who worked the land. They discovered locusts *hate* smoke!

So rather than let the locusts eat the field, the farmers learned to start a big fire. The size of the locust infestation determined the size of the fire they would kindle. If the infestation was large, the farmers would pile heaps and heaps of wood onto the fire in order to create a massive blaze with heavy, dense smoke. If the locust swarm was smaller, the situation required a smaller fire and less smoke.

As the huge fire burned, puffs of gray and black smoke from the blaze billowed upward into the sky until the air was filled with ash. Once this smoke densely filled the air, the farmer's counterattack worked! The locusts, unable to breathe, would suffocate to death and fall to the ground.

Smoke gets rid of locusts.

In a similar fashion, believers who sow God's Word into the hearts of people must learn how to deal with spiritual "locusts" — the demonic spirits who come to eat up their harvest. Just like the locusts of the air, demon spirits may allow the crop to grow for a while. They may wait to attack until the crop has begun to mature and the harvest season is imminent. Why? Because that is when they can wreak the most destruction.

> Believers who sow God's Word into the hearts of people must learn how to deal with spiritual "locusts" — the demonic spirits who come to eat up their harvest.

If we haven't suffered any spiritual attacks in a while and things appear to be going nicely, we may forget the potential threat of the enemy's strategies against us. However, *that* is often when the enemy attacks — at a time when our guard is down and we're being neglectful of our role as "watchmen on the wall."

For instance, Satan often likes to wait as churches, ministries, businesses, and personal dreams begin to grow and mature until they are finally producing their best results. Then he sends hordes of demonic spirits into the camp like a cloud of locusts descending on a field. And those evil forces have one focus: *to devour and destroy the healthy growth and forward progress of a God-given assignment.*

We must not allow ourselves to become blind to the possibility of attack. None of us is above this type of danger. Regardless of how sweet things look, how green the pasture is right now, and how promising the future looks, we must always remember: *There is an enemy out there who wants to destroy God's work!*

What should you do if demonic devourers attack your field? *Start a fire and release some Holy Ghost smoke!*

Releasing Holy Ghost smoke is the way to counterattack a demonic infestation! Never forget that Satan knows how to instigate a myriad of crises, and he can keep you running from one problem to another. Instead of worrying, fretting, and handling these attacks from man's mere point of view, we must learn how to release the smoke of the Holy Spirit to eliminate spiritual pests! As Zechariah 4:6 says, "...Not by might, nor by power, but by my spirit, saith the Lord of hosts."

TURN UP THE FIRE!

Satanic attacks on your field — your church, your ministry, your family, your business, your personal dream — must be dealt with using Holy Ghost fire and smoke. *But what is Holy Ghost smoke, and how do you release it into the atmosphere?*

The fire and smoke of the Holy Spirit is released into the spiritual atmosphere when you enter into a season of intense, Spirit-led praying. This type of prayer has the power to launch a counterattack against negative spiritual forces and supernaturally repel them out of your territory.

At first, evil forces may attempt to cling to your long-awaited harvest so they can wreak their havoc in your life. But as you press deeply and forcefully against the powers of darkness opposing you with fierce, Spirit-led prayer, those evil forces will begin to release their grip and *flee.*

Never forget the power of this analogy. *Your fervent, Spirit-led praying has the same effect in the spiritual realm that smoke had when ancient farmers built a big fire and released smoke into the atmosphere to drive away locusts.*

If the attack is small, less fire is needed to combat the opposition. But if the enemy's attack against you seems huge, you will probably need to build a bigger fire! *The greater the attack, the larger the fire that is required.*

As we enter into fervent prayer to resist the enemy's attacks, the fire of the Holy Spirit will begin blazing hotter and hotter within us. And as we release the thick, powerful "smoke of the Spirit" into the spirit realm, the demonic presence opposing us will be snuffed out and driven from our camp!

> **Never forget the power of this analogy.** *Your fervent, Spirit-led praying has the same effect in the spiritual realm that smoke had when ancient farmers built a big fire and released smoke into the atmosphere to drive away locusts.*

Let those demon spirits suffocate in God's overwhelming power as they plummet downward to their ultimate destruction in that Holy Ghost fire you've produced through prayer. In that situation, the choice lies before them. They can either flee in terror from the Holy Spirit's smoke, or they ultimately can be consumed in the fire of God's wrath. As the Scriptures proclaim, "...Our God is a consuming fire" (Hebrews 12:29).

Absolutely nothing is more effective in repelling a demonic attack than releasing a strong, hot blaze of the Holy Spirit's fire and His suffocating smoke through the power of Spirit-led prayer. This kind of Holy Spirit, prayer-produced smoke will safeguard your harvest!

GOD'S PROMISE TO YOU
AS A COMBAT-ZONE FIGHTER

Let's look again at Paul's words in Second Timothy 2:6: "The husbandman that laboureth *must be* first partaker of the fruits."

Notice the phrase "must be." It tells us that Paul was relating something that absolutely and positively *must be*. In other words, the point he was about to make is not an option — it's a *necessity*.

The phrase "must be" in Greek is the word *dei*, which always conveyed the idea of *an obligation, a necessity, a requirement, a demand,* or *a rule that should never be broken, without exception.* Given the meaning of this Greek word *dei* in Second Timothy 2:6, this portion of the verse could be translated, "*The husbandman that laboureth absolutely must be...*" or, "*The husbandman that laboureth is obligated and under command....*"

What is this demand God is making? What is the necessity spoken of here? What rule is so important, crucial, and vital that it can never be bent, modified, or altered? The remainder of the verse tells us: "The husbandman that laboureth *must be first partaker of the fruits.*"

> Absolutely nothing is more effective in repelling a demonic attack than releasing a strong, hot blaze of the Holy Spirit's fire and His suffocating smoke through the power of Spirit-led prayer.

What you find in Second Timothy 2:6 is a personal promise to you from God!

Paul said, "The husbandman that laboureth must be *first partaker of the fruits.*" In other words, God wants the committed, determined, hard-working combat-zone fighters to eat from the table of victory and enjoy the fruit of success *before* anyone else does.

This is God's promise to combat-zone fighters!

With this in mind, you can understand the entire context of Second Timothy 2:3-6 as a direct promise from God. He promises us:

"If you fight like a soldier, prepare and train like an athlete. and give your heart and soul to sowing the Word in your field like a farmer, this is what I will do for you. I am permanently fixing a rule that can never be changed, altered, or modified. It says that when your battle is over and you've proven yourself to be a good soldier; when you've exercised hard like an athlete and your spiritual competition is defeated; and when your crop begins to grow and mature before your eyes — you WILL eat before anyone else eats! I will make sure you partake of the blessings! In fact, I have decided that you will be the first partaker of the fruits. Once you've faithfully done the fighting, the training, and the hard work, it is fitting that you should taste the fruits before anyone else."

God wants you to eat and enjoy the fruit of your labors!

For example, it would be ridiculous for a local pastor to pour his life into his church and yet never taste victory or personally reap the benefits of the wonderful fruit produced as a result of his efforts. Similarly, it is unthinkable that a businessman would give his life to his business, produce a successful venture, and then never be permitted to enjoy the benefits of what he has built with his life and energies.

So God declares in this passage of Scripture that:

- Just like a Roman soldier was rewarded for fighting courageously in battle, you *will be* rewarded for your steadfast fight in the combat zone.

- Just like a Greek athlete was rewarded for his training and athletic victories, you *will be* crowned with tremendous blessings for triumphantly facing down demonic competition and adversity.

- And just as a hard-working farmer enjoys the firstfruits of his labor, you *will* eat the fruit of your labor as you work your land and labor strenuously in the combat zone to ensure that God's Word grows in your own heart and in the hearts of people.

When Do You Get Rewarded?

Although eternal rewards do await faithful Christian soldiers in the afterlife, many blessings are available and ready to be delivered to the saints *now*.

Roman soldiers didn't risk their lives so they could be killed without the hope of compensation. They did it so they could be rewarded during their lifetime!

Likewise, the Greek athletes of Timothy's day didn't do all that training, work, and preparation in order to die without reward. They were pursuing reward, and they desired gratification in *this* life for their skill and work.

Neither did farmers work their fields so their crops would fail! They planned on reaping a harvest as soon as possible. They made this their goal every year. They were after the fruit of the field, and they looked forward to personally eating it and then benefiting financially from what they had produced by their hard labor.

Many Christians struggle with the idea of being rewarded or recognized for their efforts. They ask questions like:

1. *Is it wrong to desire reward?*

2. *Is it unspiritual to want recognition for your fight?*

3. *It is selfish to reach for blessings in this life?*

4. *Is it incorrect to expect remuneration for your labors?*

The answer to all of these questions is a resounding *"No!"* That is exactly what Paul was trying to tell us. If you've done your job well, you should expect to be rewarded, recognized, blessed, and remunerated for your efforts. Anyone who lives, fights, and conquers in the combat zone *should* be rewarded.

Jesus spoke of this principle in Mark 10:29 and 30, saying:

> **...Verily I say unto you, There is no man that hath left house, or brethren, or sisters, or father, or mother, or wife, or children, or lands, for my sake, and the gospel's. But he shall receive an hundredfold now in this time, houses, and brethren, and sisters, and mothers, and children, and lands, with persecutions; and in the world to come eternal life.**

Religious thinking tries to delude us into believing that we should expect nothing in this life for our service. This thinking says that all rewards are spiritual only and bestowed only in Heaven. In fact, these same religious spirits tell us that if we expect to be rewarded now with temporal blessings for our efforts, our motives are wrong and we are in sin. This thinking also says that we should never give tithes and offerings with a thought of receiving something in return and that we should never serve in any capacity with a hidden thought of being rewarded.

However, this kind of thinking is completely wrong!

Paul said in First Corinthians 9:7-11:

> **Who goeth a warfare any time at his own charges? who planteth a vineyard, and eateth not of the fruit thereof? or who feedeth a flock, and eateth not of the milk of the flock? Say I these things as a man? or saith not the law the same also?**
>
> **For it is written in the law of Moses, Thou shalt not muzzle the mouth of the ox that treadeth out the corn. Doth God take care for oxen?**

Or saith he it altogether for our sakes? For our sakes, no doubt, this is written: that he that ploweth should plow in hope; and that he that thresheth in hope should be partaker of his hope. If we have sown unto you spiritual things, is it a great thing if we shall reap your carnal things?

Skilled warriors *deserve* blessings. Good athletes *deserve* recognition. Diligent farmers *deserve* to eat their crops. And if you are living and fighting your fight of faith in the combat zone, *you deserve a big victory.* Not only do you deserve a spiritual reward in Heaven, but you also deserve a tangible, measurable reward right now — just like any warrior, athlete, or farmer should expect!

That's why God has established this principle — that you must be rewarded for your efforts. Paul wrote, "The husbandman that laboureth *must be first partaker of the fruits."* Any other prospect would be unfair and wrong to the worker in God's Kingdom.

DID PAUL REALLY SAY THAT?

In First Corinthians 9:24, Paul wrote, "Know ye not that they which run in a race run all, but one receiveth the prize? So run, that ye may obtain."

Notice especially where Paul said, "…Run, that ye may obtain." The word "obtain" is the Greek word *katalambano*, which refers to *a conquering attitude.* It means *to grab hold of something, pull it down, subdue it, and make it your very own.* It carries the idea of *dominion.*

Paul had a conquering attitude. He was running, fighting, serving, and working in order to *obtain.* He wanted to conquer,

> Paul had a conquering attitude. He wanted to conquer, subdue, and obtain in every arena of life! His desire was *dominion* in every realm.

subdue, and obtain in every arena of life! His desire was *dominion* in every realm. What specific example did Paul use in this verse? He used *a runner* or *an athlete*. If an athlete should expect to obtain a reward, we should expect to obtain a reward as well.

In verse 25, Paul continued: "And every man that striveth for the mastery is temperate in all things. Now they do it to obtain a corruptible crown; but we an incorruptible."

> **We should expect to receive a reward for our labor — not only an incorruptible crown in Heaven, but a tangible, physical reward in this life as well.**

Notice that the athletes were temperate in order "to obtain." Were those athletes wrong to expect a reward? Absolutely not! It is simply logical that an athlete who wins a hard-won contest should be rewarded. No one would question this. Likewise, we should expect to receive a reward for our labor — not only an incorruptible crown in Heaven, but a tangible, physical reward in this life as well.

As combat-zone fighters, we are destined to enjoy the best of both worlds!

PRESCRIPTION FOR SUPERNATURAL REVELATION

As Paul comes to the end of this section of Scripture, he concludes in Second Timothy 2:7 by saying, "Consider what I say; and the Lord give thee understanding in all things."

This may indicate that Paul realized Timothy might have difficulty putting together the totality of Paul's message to him in this letter. First, Paul had exhorted him to act like a soldier. Then the apostle had quickly switched gears and told Timothy to view himself as an athlete. Then just as quickly, Paul had shifted in his example again and instructed Timothy to act like a farmer.

Imagine if you received a letter from me in which I told you to be a soldier, an athlete, and a farmer — and then I didn't stop to fully explain each point. Instead, I made these vastly different statements in the space of three sentences. It's possible you might be left with a few questions!

Paul knew he had given his spiritual son a lot to think about. That's why he said, "*Consider* what I say...."

The word "consider" is the Greek word *noieo*, which is derived from the root word *nous*, meaning *mind*. Thus, the word *noieo* ("consider") literally means *think about this* or *use your mind*. Really, the tense indicates a habitual action, so that it could read, "*Think, think, and THINK about these things.*"

It was going to take some sorting out for Timothy to comprehend everything Paul had told him. Each statement Paul made in his letter was packed full of deep meaning, dramatically different from the previous one and vital for Timothy to understand.

If Timothy read this letter from Paul too quickly, he would miss the deeper message. Therefore, Paul said, "*Think about these things. It's time to use your mind. You must ponder everything I've said to you. In fact, you need to think, think, and THINK about them.*"

Likewise, God gave you a marvelous mind, and He *wants* you to *use* it. He also wants you to yield to the work of the Holy Spirit within, who is always endeavoring to bring enlightenment, revelation, insight, and illumination to your mind.

When you use your mind to reflect on the deeper things of God, you open a door for the Holy Spirit to flood you with divine illumination. Never make the wrong assumption that you are unspiritual if you are a thinker! God gave you your brain, and He wants you to use it!

Through the years, people have frequently asked me, "How do you know so much truth from the Scriptures?" It is really quite simple. I open my Bible; pull out my study books, history books, and the Greek New Testament; and I start *thinking*. I think, think, and *think*. In fact, sometimes I think so hard, my head begins to hurt! Then as I am deep in thought, a miracle occurs! Of course I pray for divine insight, but that insight doesn't come unless I use my mind!

> **When you use your mind to reflect on the deeper things of God, you open a door for the Holy Spirit to flood you with divine illumination.**

Paul described this miracle in the second half of Second Timothy 2:7. He said, "Consider what I say; *and the Lord give thee understanding in all things.*"

In this verse, Paul gives us a prescription to receive supernatural understanding. According to Paul, we must first fill our hearts with the Word and then *think about* and *meditate on* what we have read or heard. We are to consider it, ponder it, and roll it over and over again in our minds. This is *our* part — to *bend* our minds to the Word and *focus* our thoughts on God's truths. Then as we diligently use our minds for this holy purpose, the Holy Spirit gives us *"...understanding in all things."*

In my own personal life, pondering the truths of God's Word involves prayer, meditation, and reading books pertinent to my studies. I find that as I study and deeply reflect on what is before me, a thought will abruptly come into my mind. This is often the Holy Spirit injecting my mind with understanding about the subject I am trying to gain insight on. I do my part — praying, thinking, and studying — and the Holy Spirit does His part to give me *understanding*.

The Greek word for "understanding" is the word *sunesis*. It describes *a coming together of all the parts*. What this means is that if we will use our minds, God will speak to our minds and bring all the difficult, hard-to-understand pieces of information together like the pieces of a jigsaw puzzle. And when He brings all those pieces together, we'll be able to see clearly what He has to say to us. *THAT is understanding!*

Have you ever needed vital information from God but weren't sure how to obtain it? Perhaps you had various "pieces" of the puzzle but couldn't seem to fit them together to see the whole picture. In such cases, your own human perception of God's plan was fragmented, and you couldn't make sense of it. When this happens, it's time to use your mind and *think*.

Bend your mind to the Word. Make your mind work hard, and consider what the Scriptures have to say to you. As you do your part, a supernatural understanding will begin to emerge. God will drive a thought into your mind that will put it all together for you. *He will give you understanding.*

> If we will use our minds, God will speak to our minds and bring all the difficult, hard-to-understand pieces of information together like the pieces of a jigsaw puzzle. And when He brings all those pieces together, we'll be able to see clearly what He has to say to us.

To Be an Undefeated Champion!

What does all this have to do with you? How does this relate to the combat zone you're living in right now?

You, like Timothy, must spend time meditating on and thinking about the examples Paul has given us in these verses. You won't fully comprehend them all at once, so you must decide to ponder them until you grasp their full meaning. These truths are so powerful that you simply can't meditate on them too much.

> **It's a daily choice every one of us must make — to bend our minds to God's Word and submit our thoughts to His plan.**

It's a daily choice every one of us must make — to bend our minds to God's Word and submit our thoughts to His plan. And as we do, we will begin to view ourselves as soldiers in God's army, as serious athletes in training to win every wrestling match with the enemy, and as hard-working farmers who immerse themselves fully in the work of the Lord's end-time harvest. And once we're armed with *that* victorious mindset, we will come through every contest as undefeated champions!

CHAPTER NINE

THE CHOICE IS OURS TO MAKE

All of us as believers face challenges and difficulties in life. If we are going to overcome, we must each make the decision to *fight* for what God has promised us and what He has called us to accomplish on this earth. Contending for the fullness of His plan to be fulfilled in our lives requires commitment of the highest level, and sustaining that commitment may seem difficult when we are in the midst of a combat zone. But our choice to hold fast and to keep fighting till the battle is won will always produce fruit and bring great reward.

Especially if you are weary in the midst of a sustained attack, the thought of giving up may seem like the easiest course of action to take. But if you throw in the towel and surrender, your decision will produce only defeat, sadness of spirit, and loss in many areas of your life. As difficult as it may seem to hold fast and finish the task before you, you must make the decision that you're going to defeat the odds and overcome every strategy the enemy throws at you to convince you to quit.

> Contending for the fullness of His plan to be fulfilled in our lives requires commitment of the highest level. But our choice to hold fast and to keep fighting till the battle is won will always produce fruit and bring great reward.

That determined decision will eventually produce a great victory that will spill over into every area of your life. You'll be so thankful that you didn't give up!

> **Most moments of defeat in life are produced not by any demonic attack, but by our own *lack of commitment* to stay in the fight.**

We have to continually keep in mind that the devil is a defeated foe. So although we often feel like we're defeated because of the devil's attacks being waged against us, we're often putting the blame on the wrong source. Most moments of defeat in life are produced not by any demonic attack, but by our own *lack of commitment* to stay in the fight. But when we dig in our heels, refuse to surrender, and use our authority in Jesus Christ to resist the devil, he *flees in terror* from us!

WHAT IF THE FIGHT INTENSIFIES?

If life in the combat zone intensifies and the fight grows difficult, we must be determined to fight even *harder*. Remember, Paul admonished us to "…therefore endure hardness, as a good soldier of Jesus Christ" (2 Timothy 2:3).

But can anyone *really* be the kind of soldier that Jesus Christ was while He walked on this earth? Paul answered that question as he continued in Second Timothy 2:8, saying, "Remember that Jesus Christ of the seed of David was raised from the dead according to my gospel."

There are four facets of Second Timothy 2:8 pertinent to the subject of fighting a good fight of faith:

- Remembering Jesus Christ

- Remembering Jesus' humanity

- Remembering Jesus' resurrection

- Remembering the Gospel message

Why did Paul tell Timothy to remember these four specific aspects of Jesus Christ? Because he knew that dwelling on the story of Jesus' life would encourage Timothy's heart — and it will encourage you as well.

First, Paul said, "*Remember* Jesus Christ...." The word "remember" is actually the same root word for *a grave* or *a memorial*. This is important because it implies that Timothy's accurate vision of Jesus had become blurred — perhaps even nearly buried and forgotten. In essence, Paul was saying to Timothy, *"Dig through your swamped mind like it's a grave covered with dirt, and pull out a clear vision of Jesus Christ."*

Paul exhorted Timothy to resurrect an accurate picture of Jesus Christ and then to erect this picture in his mind like a statue, monument, or memorial. Timothy needed a lasting, permanent vision of all that Jesus Christ had endured. Then Timothy needed to build a fixed image in his mind of Jesus' ultimate and everlasting victory over hell and the grave.

Why did Timothy need to do this? To encourage himself in the Lord!

'FOR THE JOY SET BEFORE HIM'

One way to encourage ourselves in the Lord is to compare our problems to the cruel trial, scourgings, and horrible death that Jesus endured. Every time we do that, the trials we're going through will always end up looking absolutely trivial in comparison.

Hebrews 12:2 relates the unimaginable suffering that Jesus endured during His ordeal on the Cross. It says, "Looking unto Jesus the author and finisher of our faith; who for the joy that was set before him endured the cross, despising the shame, and is set down at the right hand of the throne of God."

Notice this verse didn't say, *"Jesus loved hanging on the Cross, and He enjoyed the shame."* Rather, the Word says He *"endured the* cross." This word "endure" is the Greek word *hupomeno,* which denotes *a commitment to stay in one spot, regardless of how difficult the situation gets.*

In other words, the word "endure" tells us that the Cross was no joy ride! Yet in spite of it all, Jesus was committed to staying put and hanging on that horrible Cross, regardless of the personal torment it brought Him or the price He had to pay.

Hebrews 12:2 continues by telling us what Jesus thought of the Cross. It says, "...*despising* the shame...." The word "despising" is the Greek word *kataphroneo,* which means *to look down on something, to disdain an object, to feel humiliated about something, to scorn,* or *to have contempt for something.* This Greek word clearly reveals that Jesus *despised* the shame His work on the Cross brought Him; He *disdained* the *Cross* as an object of scorn; He had *contempt* for the ugliness of the assignment; and He was *humiliated* by the condemnation it brought upon Him.

> In spite of it all, Jesus was committed to staying put and hanging on that horrible Cross, regardless of the personal torment it brought Him or the price He had to pay.

The Bible goes on to say that Jesus despised the "shame." The word "shame" in Greek is the word *aischunos,* which refers to *a disgraceful predicament.* Jesus saw His public nakedness and ridicule,

His slanderous trial, and His absorption of man's sin as an unspeakable disgrace to Himself. In addition, the idea of spending three days in hell was a horrendous thought to the Son of God.

Jesus *despised* the work of the Cross — yet He went through with it. Why is this? Hebrews 12:2 tells us: Jesus did it for "...the joy that was set before him...." After He had finished His work of redemption for all mankind, Jesus was "...set down at the right hand of the throne of God."

Jesus endured all the shame and suffering of the Cross, both for us and for Himself, because He had His eyes permanently fixed on His reward. Jesus was committed to enduring the entire gamut of devilish ordeals in order to obtain His rightful place at the Father's right hand. Imagine the *joy* Jesus experienced when He broke free of hell's clutches and received that seat of highest authority!

What is the joy set before *you* today? Is it a successful church? A growing business? The salvation of certain family members? The fulfillment of what God has destined you to do?

Just like Jesus, you must keep your eyes permanently fixed on the desire God planted in your heart that pertains to your part in His plan. If your vision wavers, you will begin to lose your firm grasp on your commitment. But that is *not* the time to loosen your grip — it's the time to redouble your efforts to *hold on tight*! You must steadfastly look *forward* toward the goal God has set before you. Refuse to get distracted by any circumstance that surrounds you or any negative emotion or thought that would try to derail you!

Jesus fixed His sight on the joy of the glory that lay before Him, and that confident hope *enabled* Him to endure the Cross and its shame. Therefore, let Jesus be your example, and keep your eyes fixed on the joy set before *you*!

JESUS KNOWS HOW TO TRIUMPH!

In order to fully grasp the sensation of victory that Jesus Himself experienced when He conquered all His enemies, let's look at Colossians 2:15. It says, "And having spoiled principalities and powers, he [Jesus] made a shew of them openly, triumphing over them in it."

> You must steadfastly look *forward* toward the goal God has set before you. Refuse to get distracted by any circumstance that surrounds you or any negative emotion or thought that would try to derail you!

This is what I call a graphic verse. It is a picture painted for us by the Holy Spirit — a gorgeous, vivid illustration of the day Jesus defeated death, hell, and the grave!

Understanding the phrase "triumphing over them in it" is the key to fully grasping the layers of meaning found in this verse. This phrase is derived from the Greek word *triambeuo*, which is a word used to describe *a conqueror or general returning home from a grand victory in enemy territory*. The word "triumph" was a specific word used to describe this *triumphal parade*.

In ancient Roman society when news reached Rome that the emperor or the commander of his army had defeated an enemy, plans for a triumphal parade were immediately drawn up. By the time the victorious emperor or commander returned home, the people were ready and eager to celebrate his victory. As the city gates swung open and the imperial ruler or general rode through on his handsome steed, *the celebration began*!

If it was the emperor, he would stand in his chariot pulled by magnificent horses, draped in his regal, kingly garments and wearing a shining royal crown upon his head. As this triumphant ruler rode purposefully down the city's main avenue, his people would begin rejoicing, dancing, and singing in jubilation. This was a time to rejoice! The entire city would line the streets in a procession of celebration and victory as the emperor rode through his city with his head held high, his shoulders thrown back, and a look of victory on his face. This joyous procession was called a "triumphal parade."

In order to flaunt his great victory, the emperor or commander would also parade his defeated foes through the city. The vanquished foreign king, bound in heavy chains, would be forced to walk laboriously behind the imperial chariot. The deposed king's defeated nobles and generals would follow, also bound in heavy chains. Further back in the procession, servants would pull oxcarts overflowing with booty taken by force from the enemy's homeland. These goods had once belonged to the enemy, but now they belonged to the conquering emperor!

As the victorious ruler or general rode down the main avenue, he flaunted his defeated foes, and "made a show of them openly." He wanted everyone to see the fabulous goods he had stolen from his enemy's land. He wanted his people to know that their enemy had been completely "spoiled."

However, the story doesn't stop here!

After the returning ruler or commander had ridden down the main avenue, displaying his spoils of war while the masses sang his song of victory, he'd reach a large set of stairs that led upward to a huge platform. His military conquest had proven that he still held the ultimate authority. Therefore, he would proudly walk up the steps, turn toward the crowd, and make the great announcement that victory had been achieved!

This picture I have just described is the backdrop to Colossians 2:15, which says, "And having spoiled principalities and powers, he made a shew of them openly, triumphing over them in it." This was "the joy that was set before" Jesus! After He had conquered death, hell, and the grave, Jesus returned home to Heaven where a celebratory, triumphal parade took place in His honor! And who led that celestial parade? The Great Victor, Jesus Christ!

Imagine the worship, praise, and adoration that took place on the day that Jesus, our reigning King, returned home to the glory of Heaven to sit down at the Father's right hand! That grand victory was the reason Jesus could "endure the cross." He didn't enjoy the shame; He *despised* it. However, His eternal reward far outweighed the temporal, momentary suffering of the Cross.

REMEMBER, REMEMBER, REMEMBER...

Paul's command to Timothy in Second Timothy 2:8 was to "remember Jesus Christ." The Greek tense used indicates that Paul was emphatically saying to the younger minister, "I *command* you to remember Jesus Christ...."

Likewise, you may be currently enduring a situation that you despise. You know you are called to your place of ministry, business, or some other place of assignment; you are certain that you're *exactly* where God wants you to be. Yet despite this assurance, all hell seems to be breaking out around you, and you have plenty of natural, rational reasons to back out and retreat.

Rather than giving up, however, you must *stay the course* and "*remember Jesus Christ.*" Take time to reflect on the Author and

Finisher of your faith — the trial He endured, the Cross He despised, the disgrace He felt, and the phenomenal victory He won.

As Hebrews 12:3 says, "…Consider him that endured such contradiction of sinners against himself, lest ye be wearied and faint in your minds." The word "consider" in this verse is the Greek word *analogidzomai*, which means *to think again* or *to reflect on that subject one more time*. It conveys the idea of *habitual meditation*, and it is also written in the imperative tense, which means it is a *command*. Given the imperative tense of this Greek word, it could be actually translated: *"Think, think, and think again. Reflect on this subject one more time. Don't stop; rather, do it habitually. In fact, I command you to do this!"*

How does this idea of habitual meditation relate in the context of Hebrews 12:3? By constantly meditating on Jesus Christ and all He "endured," we are inwardly strengthened to face our own fight of faith. The word "endure" in this verse is *hupomeno*, the same Greek word used in Hebrews 12:2, and it again indicates *a commitment to stay in one spot, regardless of how difficult the situation gets.*

By using this word a *second* time, the Holy Spirit laid a special emphasis on this particular point. He wants us to know that the Cross was not enjoyable for Jesus; it was something that had to be "endured." Yet because it was part of Jesus' necessary journey to win the war for our lives, He endured it. The experience was unspeakably horrific, but Jesus was committed to stay on that Cross, regardless of how difficult it became. Thank God for Jesus' relentless commitment!

There is another extremely important point found in Hebrews 12:3. The Word continues, "For consider him that endured such *contradiction* of sinners against himself…." Notice the word "contradiction." In Greek, it is the word *antilogia*, which is a compound of the two words *anti* and *logia*. The word *anti* means *against*, and it conveys the idea of *hostility*. The word *logia* simply means *words*. When these two Greek words are compounded, the new word literally means *angry, hostile, and cruel words*.

This tells us that when Jesus took His greatest step of faith and literally laid His life on the altar of sacrifice, *that* is when His most slanderous persecution arose! Luke 23:35-37,39 records the slander Jesus received as He hung on the Cross:

> **And the people stood beholding. And the rulers also with them derided him, saying, He saved others; let him save himself, if he be the Christ, the chosen of God. And the soldiers also mocked him...saying, if thou be the king of the Jews, save thyself.... And one of the malefactors which were hanged railed on him, saying, If thou be Christ, save thyself and us."**

In Jesus' greatest hour of pain, what did He receive? People's insults, mockery, and derision!

A FIGHT ALWAYS FOLLOWS ILLUMINATION

Have you ever felt like you were being talked about, laughed at, or railed on because of your fight of faith? If so, you can know that you're doing something right! In fact, Hebrews 10:32 says all faithful fighters experience this kind of ridicule: "But call to remembrance the former days, in which, after ye were illuminated, ye endured a great fight of afflictions."

Notice the word "illuminated" in this verse. It is the Greek word *photidzo*, which refers to *light, enlightenment*, or *fresh revelation*. It is the Greek word from which we derive the root in "photograph." The idea contained within this Greek word is that the new illumination or light is so powerful that it leaves a *permanent, lasting impression on person's life*.

Can you remember when you were first "illuminated" concerning the infilling of the Holy Spirit? Did it feel like someone suddenly "turned the light on" for you? Did it leave a lasting mark on your life?

Do you remember when you heard for the first time that Jesus Christ took your infirmities and carried your diseases? Do you recall how your spirit seemed to burst forth with joy? Did it leave a permanent impression on your life? You felt that way because you had been "illuminated."

Perhaps you can recall the day when you were first called into the ministry. What happened to you? Were you overwhelmed, filled with joy, and forever changed? In that instance, the Holy Spirit "illuminated" you about the call of God.

True "illumination" from the Holy Spirit makes a strong, indelible mark on our lives. It forever changes us. And that is a very good thing, too, because of what the Word says follows "illumination." Hebrews 10:32 tells us: "…After ye were illuminated, *ye endured a great fight of afflictions.*" According to the Word of God, a *fight* always follows illumination!

> **Hebrews 10:32 tells us: "…After ye were illuminated, *ye endured a great fight of afflictions.*" According to the Word of God, a *fight* always follows illumination!**

In this verse, the word "endured" is once again the word *hupomeno*, which indicates *a commitment to stay in one spot, regardless of how difficult the situation gets.* This tells us that no matter how difficult our fight becomes, we must make the decision to stand in faith and be immovable in our commitment.

Next, the Bible says we must endure "*a great fight of afflictions.*" There are three important words to take note of in this phrase: "great," "fight," and "afflictions."

First, the word "great" is the Greek word *mega*, which describes *something very, very large.* The word *mega* speaks of *enlargement.* That is why people speak of "*mega*-bills," "*mega*-problems," "*mega*-work," and so forth. By using this word, Hebrews 12:3 is telling us the fight that follows illumination is not typically small — it is *mega.*

The next important word in the phrase is the word "fight." This is the Greek word *athlesis,* which refers to *a committed athlete,* just like the Greek athletes we saw in Chapter Seven. In the context of this verse, this word *athlesis* conveys the message that real, powerful illumination may throw you into the greatest challenge of your entire life!

Finally, we come to the word "afflictions," which is the Greek word *pathema.* This word *pathema* primarily refers to *mental pressure* or *suffering that affects the mind.* This is *not* a reference to mental sickness; rather, it refers to *a fight of faith, a war in your soul,* or *an attack on your mind.*

One thing is certain: If you take a stand in faith, every possible negative thought will come against your mind! This is exactly happened to Jesus on the Cross. After yielding to the work of the Cross and selflessly giving His own life, the soldiers and other criminals began to throw "contradictions" at Him.

Because the Lord Jesus was human as well as divine, you can be sure that He was tempted to listen to their accusations. However, Jesus shoved aside the demonic attack in His soul and endured — *staying in His place on the Cross, no matter how difficult the fight became.*

Have you ever been through a *mega-ordeal?* Have you ever been thrown into *the greatest fight of your life?* Do you know what it is like to withstand *an all-out assault on your mind?*

If so, it probably means that somewhere along your spiritual journey, you have been *illuminated*. If there were no illumination, there would likely be no challenge. That fight is almost certain evidence you're on the right track.

You're on Center Stage

In Hebrews 10:33, the Word continues, "Partly, whilst ye were made a gazingstock both by reproaches and afflictions...." Notice the word "gazingstock." It is the Greek word *theatron*, which refers to *a theater*. A better translation might read, *"You were made a theater..."; "You became a spectacle of entertainment...";* or, *"On account of your stance of faith, you became the best show in town...."*

This word paints the picture of spectators taking a seat at the theater to see a play and then watching the entire show. However, instead of watching the show to appreciate it, the audience is watching attentively in the hopes of catching the actors *making a mistake*. The crowd is on the edge of their seats, anticipating the first mistake, forgotten line, or error on the part of the actors. When they finally hear a mistake, they intend to laugh at the player and make fun of him, scorning and ridiculing him.

By using this Greek word, the writer of Hebrews was telling us that this kind of scorn *always* accompanies a determined stance of faith. There are always spectators who stand by, ready to laugh at you or to say, "We told you so!" when you make

> Have you ever been thrown into *the greatest fight of your life?* If so, it probably means that somewhere along your spiritual journey, you have been *illuminated*. That fight is almost certain evidence you're on the right track.

your first mistake in your walk of faith. Sadly, many times these scornful spectators are not unbelievers, but *believers*!

When you take a step of faith or take a new stand on the Word of God — *when you are first illuminated* — it will throw you into the public eye whether you like it or not. You may not be known by thousands of people, but your life will become dinner conversation among friends, family, associates, and foes. Everyone will seem to develop an opinion regarding whether or not you'll be able to fulfill your dream.

Hebrews 10:33 contains two other very important words that are relevant to this discussion — the words "reproaches" and "afflictions."

The word "reproach" is the Greek word *oneidismos*, which refers to *insults hurled at you from other people*. This is precisely the kind of insults the soldiers hurled at Jesus when He hung on the Cross. That Cross put Jesus on the center stage of the universe. Rather than applauding Him, the spectators "reproached" Him by throwing insults and slanderous statements at Him.

Satan hates it when you stand strong on God's Word. He will do everything within his ability to knock you off your stance of faith. He will use family members, friends, associates, and circumstances to thwart the plan of God for your life. However, once you are "illuminated" regarding God's perfect will for you, you must determine that you won't budge an *inch* off the path of pursuing His will — regardless of any demonic opposition you encounter!

The other word to take note of in verse 33 is the word "afflictions." This is a different Greek word than the one used in verse 32. Here the word "afflictions" is the word *thlipsis*, which refers to *a tight squeeze* or *incredible pressure*. This is the kind of pressure that life puts on you.

It's bad enough to have revilers come against you, but it says here that when you take a stance of faith, *life itself* will try to come against you. The word *thlipsis* indicates that when you are illuminated, *everything around you will try to shut you down.*

You see, the devil hates the illumination in your heart, and he hates you because you are illuminated. Therefore, the problems he brings against you are not indicators that you're doing something wrong. Rather, they are telltale signs that you're doing something *right* — something that Satan absolutely can't stand!

Why is "illumination" so terrifying to Satan? Because an illuminated person is a dangerous person! *Such a person knows the will of God for his life with absolute certainty — and he doesn't care if anyone else in the world agrees with him or not!* This is a person whom religious politics cannot buy and Satan cannot stop.

> Once you are "illuminated" regarding God's perfect will for you, you must determine that you won't budge an *inch* off the path of pursuing His will — regardless of any demonic opposition you encounter!

Spiritual illumination is a powerful force. A believer who has been illuminated will stand in faith against all the odds, and he will *beat* them! He will oppose the opinion of the entire world if he must, because *he knows* he's right!

However, you must know in advance that *a fight will always follow illumination.*

'LEST YE BE WEARIED...'

Hebrews 12:3 gives us a reason why we must constantly stay in remembrance of Jesus and this truth that a fight always follows illumination. It says, "...Consider him that endured such contradiction of sinners against himself, *lest ye be wearied and faint in your minds.*" The word "weary" in this verse is the word *kamete*, which describes *someone who is slowly being worn out.* This kind of individual has tried and tried to remain true, but he is slowly becoming *spiritually depleted.*

Also, take note of the next significant word in this verse — the word "faint." This word tells us what will happen *if* we give in to weariness. It is the Greek word *ekluomai*, which is a compound of the two words *ek* and *luo. Ek* means *out*, and *luo* means *to loosen* or *lose.* In fact, the word *luo* is used in Luke 3:16 where John the Baptist said of Jesus, "...the latchet of whose shoes I am not worthy *to unloose....*" The word "unloose" in this verse is the same word *luo*, which in this context means *to loosen so that the shoes slip right off.*

> Spiritual illumination is a powerful force. A believer who has been illuminated will stand in faith against all the odds, and he will *beat* them! He will oppose the opinion of the entire world if he must, because *he knows* he's right!

When the words *ek* and *luo* are compounded, the new word describes *an individual so weary, tired, and exhausted that he literally goes limp.* It is a picture of total defeat.

Spiritual burnout is a real possibility for any believer. It is certainly possible to become so spiritually depleted that you no longer care if you win or lose. However, you do not have to accept this as an option in your life. God has a better way! Instead of burning out and succumbing to defeat and apathy, do as the Word exhorts and "...*consider him....*"

When you become exhausted and tired of living in the combat zone, stop and think again about Jesus Himself! When you consider Him — His trials and His victory over death, hell, and the grave — your heart will grow strong again, and you will be ready to keep fighting your fight of faith.

Remember the Resurrection

In Second Timothy 2:8, Paul continued his message to Timothy by saying, "Remember that Jesus Christ *of the seed of David....*" What is the significance of Paul specifically pointing out that Jesus was "of the seed of David?" Paul was placing emphasis on *the humanity* of Jesus Christ.

By referencing Jesus' family lineage, Paul was essentially saying, *"Jesus Christ defeated death, hell, and the grave, not in the power of His divinity, but as a Man while He was still the seed of David."* This statement is important because it negates the argument: "Jesus was able to endure hardness and emerge victorious only because He was God." Paul attacked that kind of thinking before it even had a chance to take root. Paul made his message clear: Although Jesus Christ *was* God, His incredible victory over Satan was won while He was still *"of the seed of David."*

This is very significant to us. This means that because Jesus could face His trials, scourgings, mockery, Cross, humiliation, and death in the weak power of the flesh as a *Man* and still be victorious, we also can face our combat zone and come out as victors!

Therefore, we have *no* excuses. We can't blame our defeat on anyone else or say that it was impossible for us to win. Jesus was up against incomprehensible odds, yet He remained faithful to His calling and accomplished His task!

Jesus defeated Satan as a Man, and so can you!

In verse 8, Paul immediately continued, "Remember that Jesus Christ of the seed of David was *raised from the dead.*" Jesus didn't stay dead; He arose! Thank God, death was not Jesus' final destiny.

And God's ultimate plan for your life is resurrection and victory as well! Just as Jesus was raised from the dead as the living Lord and Victor, God intends for you to move out of the combat zone into a broad, abundant place of victory over every trial and temptation you face!

> **Just as Jesus was raised from the dead as the living Lord and Victor, God intends for you to move out of the combat zone into a broad, abundant place of victory over every trial and temptation you face!**

Don't allow the enemy to lie to you and tell you that you are assigned to a life of perpetual fighting. Such thinking will only discourage your heart.

We're not fighting for the sake of *fighting* — we are fighting for the purpose of *winning!*

Don't become so swamped in your troubles that they become the totality of what you can see. If you do, you will only find yourself wallowing in discouragement and self-defeat. Remember, Jesus Christ was raised from the dead, and just like Jesus, you have a wonderful future ahead of you.

Don't give up now. *There is life beyond the combat zone!*

DO IT FOR THE SAKE OF THE GOSPEL

In the last portion of Second Timothy 2:8, Paul said, "Remember that Jesus Christ of the seed of David was raised from the dead *according to my gospel.*" Paul concluded this verse by talking about the Gospel message.

Paul was essentially telling Timothy, *"Timothy, if you can't remain true for any other reason, remain true for the Gospel's sake."* And just like the rest of Paul's message to Timothy, this instruction applies to us as well. Remaining true for the Gospel's sake must be the bottom line for all of us.

There were people in Timothy's church who were looking to him as their example. They were watching to see how their "fearless leader" would respond to the problems around him. He was their primary example to follow and imitate. If Timothy forsook the Lord like others had done, it would have discredited the Gospel message in his church and in the city of Ephesus. That's why Paul essentially told him, *"Timothy, if you can't remain faithful for any other reason, do it for those who are watching. Do it for the sake of the Gospel!"*

> **We're not fighting for the sake of *fighting* — we are fighting for the purpose of *winning!***

Likewise, you need to be aware that people are constantly watching you. Those same people who heard you make your confession of faith are watching you to see if you are *serious.* They are waiting to see if your "faith walk" is *real* or if it is just a *passing whim.* Your example will either *prove* the Gospel to them or *discredit* it completely. *What are you going to do?*

Many preachers have prophesied great things that God was going to do through their church. Yet because of adversity or a lack of finances, they backed off and ceased to pursue the vision God gave them. What a disgrace this is to the Gospel! It brings ridicule and shame upon the preaching of the Word.

If you can't remain true for any other reason, do it for the sake of the Gospel. If you can't remain true for any temporal reason, then remain true for *eternal* reasons.

You can be the deciding factor between Heaven and hell for some people! By your own witness of the truth and your stance of faith on the Scriptures, you can make the difference between divine healing or premature death for others. Never diminish your importance as a signpost to the truth of the Gospel message. People are watching your life. *This matter is too critical to ignore!*

We must never, ever lose sight of this crucial consideration. If for no other reason, we must remain faithful for the sake of the Gospel and for those who need to hear the truth and be rescued from an eternity without God!

> **Never diminish your importance as a signpost to the truth of the Gospel message. People are watching your life.**

That is why Paul continued in Second Timothy 2:9 by saying, "Wherein I suffer trouble, as an evil doer, even unto bonds; but the word of God is not bound."

The Gospel was the reason Paul was imprisoned and soon to be martyred for his faith. When he wrote, "Wherein I suffer trouble...," he was actually saying, *"This Gospel is why I suffer trouble."* Yet his victorious attitude is evident as he concluded with the stirring declaration: "...But the word of God *is not bound.*"

Rather than surrendering to his vile predicament, Paul *used* it to the Gospel's advantage. From his prison cell, he couldn't preach to crowds anymore, but he *could* write letters!

God is able to turn anything around! Most of Paul's letters were written as a result of satanic attacks that landed him in prison. Because he couldn't physically visit the churches under his spiritual supervision, he addressed them by letter. *Paul didn't allow the enemy's attack to prevent him from fulfilling his heavenly assignment.*

Don't surrender to the adversary's attacks. *The choice is yours to make; therefore, be certain to make the right choice.* Decide to *conquer*. Decide to *win*! Decide to use any satanic attack that comes against you as a steppingstone to further the Gospel!

This was Paul's attitude. Concerning his frequent imprisonments, he wrote:

> **But I would ye should understand, brethren, that the things which happened unto me have fallen out rather unto the furtherance of the gospel; so that my bonds in Christ are manifest in all the palace, and in all other places.**
>
> **Philippians 1:12,13**

Paul could have cried, "Foul play!" He could have sobbed, "This doesn't line up with my theology! Why did God permit this to happen to me?" Yet instead of getting bogged down in this kind of mental muck, Paul chose to rise above the adversity and to use the trials he faced as opportunities to further the Gospel. He made *a decision* to live in victory!

And if Paul couldn't remain true for himself or for other temporal reasons, he knew he must remain true for *eternal reasons*. The Early Church looked to him for leadership, and there were still many lost people who had yet to receive Jesus as their Savior. Paul had to *decide* to walk in victory *for them*.

> Don't surrender to the adversary's attacks. *The choice is yours to make; therefore, be certain to make the right choice.* Decide to *conquer*. Decide to *win*!

Thus, in Second Timothy 2:10, Paul proclaimed, "...I endure all things for the elect's sakes, that they may also obtain the salvation which is in Christ Jesus with eternal glory."

A SONG FOR WARRIORS

Have you ever wondered what worship services of the First Century Church were like? How did they conduct their praise and worship? How did they take offerings? How did they pray for the sick? How loudly did they pray in tongues? How did they flow with the gifts of the Holy Spirit? Imagine the vitality and *life* that must have filled their church services!

As we come to the end of Paul's message on warfare, we get a glimpse of those early services. In fact, Paul concluded his message with an actual hymn that the early believers sang when they met together to worship. This early worship song, however, sounds quite different from the songs we sing today.

Second Timothy 2:11-13 is what scholars call "hymnic literature." In other words, these verses are actual lyrics from a real New Testament hymn. When hymnic literature is used in the New Testament, it is borrowed from a hymn that was well known throughout the Church. These hymns were intended to be more than music; they were tools of instruction that chronicled the very thought processes of the Early Church.

Paul quotes this familiar hymn, which says:

It is a faithful saying: For if we be dead with him, we shall also live with him:

If we suffer, we shall also reign with him: if we deny him, he also will deny us:

If we believe not, yet he abideth faithful: he cannot deny himself.

2 Timothy 2:11-13

Let's look at the first line of this song: "It is a faithful saying: For if we be dead with him, we shall also live with him...."

Can you imagine getting together in church to sing about *martyrdom*? This was not allegorical speech — this was *reality* for the early believers! Persecution and death were so prevalent to First Century Christians that they actually sang about these subjects in their worship services.

In order to prepare themselves to be able to withstand satanic attacks and live bravely for the Lord, these early believers used every tool available to them to instill bravery into their ranks. Hymns were one such tool.

'IF WE BE DEAD WITH HIM...'

As we see in Second Timothy 2:11, the first line of the song goes, "...If we be dead with him...." The phrase "if we be dead with him" comes from the Greek word *sunapothnesko*, which refers to *a literal partnership in death with someone else*. Therefore, the first line of this hymn could actually be translated, *"If we join Him as a full-fledged partner in death...."*

Imagine trying to put *that* message to music! Better yet, imagine a pastor trying to teach those lines to his congregation today! Do you think the pop Christian radio stations would give that song much air time?

The song goes on to say, "...We shall also live with him...." This phrase is based on the Greek word *sudzao*, which once again conveys the idea of *partnership*. This line of the hymn could be translated, *"We will join with Him in the same kind of supernatural life He now lives."*

This hymn was battle cry, a song of warfare and victory! Singing it over and over again worked bravery and resilience into the fiber of the Early Church!

We still need songs today that produce brave warriors. It is my dream that the Church today can be committed enough to sing this type of song *and* actually *mean* it. That would be rock-solid evidence that the army of the Lord was marching forth to victory!

> **We still need songs today that produce brave warriors.**

Yet instead of earnestly singing these powerful lyrics from the depths of their hearts, many believers today would be offended by the message and probably just refuse to sing along. Others would claim the lyrics were filled with doubt and unbelief. But these mindsets are completely wrong. These lines do not represent doubt and unbelief; they represent *powerful faith*.

The lyrics of this New Testament hymn proclaim, "Come hell or high water, we're in this army to stay! If they kill us, we still come out the victors because we'll join Jesus in His glorious resurrection!"

'IF WE SUFFER...'

The song continues with the line, "...If we suffer, we shall also reign with him...." The phrase "if we suffer" in Greek once again unites us to Jesus Christ in a *partnership*. Literally translated, it means, *"If we join Him in His suffering and suffer the same way He did...."*

Notice there is no note of sorrow or pain in this song about the early believers' suffering. Feeling sorry for themselves and wallowing in a mire of self-pity wouldn't change the situation. Therefore, they faced their challenges bravely in the power of the Spirit.

Although these early believers didn't seek out suffering, they were not afraid to suffer *if* it was forced upon them because of their faith. Their worship songs were the victorious proclamations of a *fearless* people. They were determined to have victory, no matter what the cost!

When these early New Testament Christians boldly sang out, "...We shall also reign with him," the phrase "reign with him" was the Greek word *sumbasileuo*. This Greek word literally means *we will reign and rule like nobility with Him*. They had their sights fixed on *ruling with Jesus*, and in order to do this, they would fight any foe.

> Although these early believers didn't seek out suffering, they were not afraid to suffer *if* it was forced upon them because of their faith. Their worship songs were the victorious proclamations of a *fearless* people.

'IF WE DENY HIM...'

The next line of the songs reveals the dire consequences of giving up the fight. It says, "...If we deny him, he also will deny us...."

Can you imagine looking someone straight in the eyes to sing to them, "If you deny the Lord, the Lord will deny you too"?

Early believers had an attitude about serving the Lord that is sadly missing from much of the Church today. To them, there was no room for excuses or defectors in the army of the Lord.

A person was either with Jesus or against Him. There was no in-between. Furthermore, when a brother defected, they didn't sweep his desertion under the carpet and try to ignore it.

THE EARLY CHURCH WAS AN *ARMY*!

Christians who go "Absent Without Leave" (AWOL) from God's army are not worthy of honor or special privileges. Yet in the Church today, we often comfort defectors.

If a brother or a sister has fallen into sin or been hurt by a relationship, we should certainly do all we can to restore him or her. But if any leaders rebel and make a deliberate, conscious decision to defect, we should let them defect. If they later return to the Church, they should be made to start from the beginning and prove themselves.

This kind of militant lack of tolerance was starkly evident in this New Testament hymn, which declared, "...If we deny Him, the Lord will also deny us...." This is not so much a theological statement as it is a reflection of who these early believers were at their core and how they viewed their fight in the combat zone.

Christian songs are always influenced by the type of preaching, teaching, and prophesying that is taking place within the Church. As such, they are indicative of the specific period in which they are written. The author of this hymn, whoever he or she was, chronicled the messages that were prevalent in the Church at the time and put them to music so that the saints at large could sing them at home, at work, in their leisure time, or at church gatherings.

From the content of the New Testament hymn, it is clear that the early saints were extremely serious about their role in the Kingdom of God. Their Christian walk wasn't just "another thing" for them to do in life. Jesus was their "all-in-all," and they gave their lives completely to His cause. This hymn was a dramatic reflection of their day and age — and their sold-out hearts for Him.

The Choice Is Ours To Make

God is speaking to us in militaristic terms and showing us that we are to be an advancing army upon the dominions of this world. He is releasing a spirit of *war* inside the Church, calling us to pick up our knowledge, gifts, and weaponry and to *use* them against the enemy.

The most exciting days of the Church are not behind us — they are *ahead* of us! In the decades to come, we will see the kingdoms of this world clash against the Kingdom of God. Even now, this clash is beginning to manifest in a variety of ways.

> God is showing us that we are to be an advancing army upon the dominions of this world. He is releasing a spirit of *war* inside the Church, calling us to pick up our knowledge, gifts, and weaponry and to *use* them against the enemy.

As time inexorably advances toward the Second Coming of the Lord Jesus, this clash will become more pronounced, and warfare and opposition will inevitably break out across the world. It will be up to us — the brave spiritual warriors living in the combat zone — to hear God's voice, prepare ourselves to fight, and courageously step out into the spirit realm to do battle with the mighty power of the Holy Ghost.

- Are *you* ready for this battle?
- Are *you* flowing with what the Spirit of God is doing on the earth in this day?

- Are *you* listening to the voice of your Leader?

- Are *you* warring right now like as a good soldier of Jesus Christ?

- Are *you* training yourself now to become strong in spirit?

- Are *you* being faithful to the task God has given you to fulfill?

Our Commander-in-Chief is urging us to move forward, and there is no place more exciting — or dangerous — than the front lines of battle!

Today — *right now* — God needs a special brand of believers to boldly challenge the kingdom of darkness in the authority and dominion of Jesus Christ and to *storm* the gates of hell! He is looking for those special believers who will hear His voice, surrender to His call, and willingly enter the combat zone to do battle for the cause of His Kingdom.

> God is looking for those special believers who will hear His voice, surrender to His call, and willingly enter the combat zone to do battle for the cause of His Kingdom.

God is calling *you* to step ahead of the ranks, face the enemy head-on resist him, and drive him back. However, your success in the combat zone begins with a rock-solid decision to surrender your life with the very deepest kind of commitment to this holy call.

Are you among the ranks of those who willingly say yes to this heavenly call to duty? *Will you answer God's call to fight in the combat zone as a champion for His cause?*

REFERENCE BOOK LIST

1. *How To Use New Testament Greek Study Aids* by Walter Jerry Clark (Loizeaux Brothers).

2. *Strong's Exhaustive Concordance of the Bible* by James H. Strong.

3. *The Interlinear Greek-English New Testament* by George Ricker Berry (Baker Book House).

4. *The Englishman's Greek Concordance of the New Testament* by George Wigram (Hendrickson).

5. *New Thayer's Greek-English Lexicon of the New Testament* by Joseph Thayer (Hendrickson).

6. *The Expanded Vine's Expository Dictionary of New Testament Words* by W. E. Vine (Bethany).

7. *New International Dictionary of New Testament Theology* (*DNTT*); Colin Brown, editor (Zondervan).

8. *Theological Dictionary of the New Testament* (*TDNT*) by Geoffrey Bromiley; Gephard Kittle, editor (Eerdmans Publishing Co.).

9. *The New Analytical Greek Lexicon*; Wesley Perschbacher, editor (Hendrickson).

10. *The Linguistic Key to the Greek New Testament* by Fritz Rienecker and Cleon Rogers (Zondervan).

11. *Word Studies in the Greek New Testament* by Kenneth Wuest, 4 Volumes (Eerdmans).

12. *New Testament Words* by William Barclay (Westminster Press).

ABOUT THE AUTHOR

Rick Renner is a prolific author and a highly respected Bible teacher and leader in the international Christian community. Rick is the author of more than 30 books, including the bestsellers *Dressed To Kill* and *Sparkling Gems From the Greek 1 and 2*, which have sold more than 3 million copies combined.

In 1991, Rick and his family moved to what is now the former Soviet Union. Today he is the senior pastor of the Moscow Good News Church and the founder of Media Mir, the first Christian television network in the former USSR that today broadcasts the Gospel to countless Russian-speaking and English-speaking viewers around the world via multiple satellites and the Internet. He is also the founder and president of Rick Renner Ministries, based in Tulsa, Oklahoma, and host to his TV program that is seen around the world. Rick and his wife and lifelong ministry partner, Denise, lead this amazing work with the help of their sons and committed leadership team.

CONTACT RENNER MINISTRIES

For further information
about RENNER Ministries, please contact
the RENNER Ministries office nearest you,
or visit the ministry website at
www.renner.org.

**ALL USA
CORRESPONDENCE:**
RENNER Ministries
P. O. Box 702040
Tulsa, OK 74170-2040
(918) 496-3213
Or 1-800-RICK-593
Email: renner@renner.org
Website: www.renner.org

MOSCOW OFFICE:
RENNER Ministries
P. O. Box 789
101000, Russia, Moscow
+7 (495) 727-14-67
Email: partner@rickrenner.ru
Website: www.ignc.org

RIGA OFFICE:
RENNER Ministries
Unijas 99
Riga LV-1084, Latvia
+371 67802150
Email: info@goodncws.lv

KIEV OFFICE:
RENNER Ministries
P. O. Box 300
01001, Ukraine, Kiev
+38 (044) 451-8115
Email: partner@rickrenner.ru

OXFORD OFFICE:
RENNER Ministries
Box 7, 266 Banbury Road
Oxford OX2 7DL, England
+44 (0) 1865 355509
Email: europe@renner.org

SPARKLING GEMS FROM THE GREEK 1

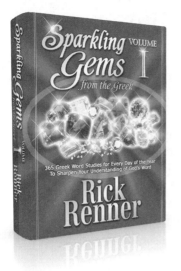

In 2003, Rick Renner's *Sparkling Gems From the Greek 1* quickly gained widespread recognition for its unique illumination of the New Testament through more than 1,000 Greek word studies in a 365-day devotional format. Today *Sparkling Gems 1* remains a beloved resource that has spiritually strengthened believers worldwide. As many have testified, the wealth of truths within its pages never grows old. Year after year, *Sparkling Gems 1* continues to deepen readers' understanding of the Bible.

$34.97 (Hardback)
1,048 pages

To order, visit us online at: **www.renner.org**

SPARKLING GEMS FROM THE GREEK 2

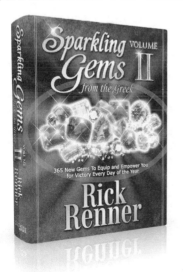

Now Rick infuses into *Sparkling Gems From the Greek 2* the added strength and richness of 13 more years of his own personal study and growth in God — expanding this devotional series to impact the reader's heart on a deeper level than ever before. This remarkable study tool helps unlock new hidden treasures from God's Word that will draw readers into an ever more passionate pursuit of Him.

$49.97 (Hardback)
1,280 pages

To order, visit us online at: **www.renner.org**

A BIBLICAL APPROACH TO SPIRITUAL WARFARE

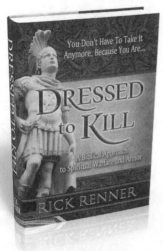

Rick Renner's book *Dressed To Kill* is considered by many to be a true classic on the subject of spiritual warfare. The original version, which sold more than 400,000 copies, is a curriculum staple in Bible schools worldwide. In this beautifully bound hardback volume, you will find:

- 512 pages of reedited text

- 16 pages of full-color illustrations

- Questions at the end of each chapter to guide you into deeper study

$24.97 (Hardback)
ISBN: 978-0-9779459-0-0

In *Dressed To Kill*, Rick explains with exacting detail the purpose and function of each piece of Roman armor. In the process, he describes the significance of our *spiritual* armor not only to withstand the onslaughts of the enemy, but also to overturn the tendencies of the carnal mind. Furthermore, Rick delivers a clear, scriptural presentation on the biblical definition of spiritual warfare — what it is and what it is not.

When you walk with God in deliberate, continual fellowship, He will enrobe you with Himself. Armed with the knowledge of who you are in Him, you will be dressed and dangerous to the works of darkness, unflinching in the face of conflict, and fully equipped to take the offensive and gain mastery over any opposition from your spiritual foe. You don't have to accept defeat anymore once you are *dressed to kill*!

To order, visit us online at: **www.renner.org**

Book Resellers: Contact Harrison House at 800-888-4126 or visit **www.HarrisonHouse.com** for quantity discounts.

BOOKS BY RICK RENNER

Dream Thieves*
Dressed To Kill*
The Holy Spirit and You* (formerly titled, *The Dynamic Duo*)
How To Receive Answers From Heaven*
Insights to Successful Leadership
Jesus' Message to the Church of Pergamum**
   (Vol. 10 in the Light in Darkness eBook series)
Life in the Combat Zone*
A Light in Darkness, Volume One
The Love Test*
No Room for Compromise, A Light in Darkness, Volume Two
Paid in Full*
The Point of No Return*
Repentance*
Say Yes!* (formerly titled, *If You Were God, Would You Choose You?*)
Seducing Spirits and Doctrines of Demons
Sparkling Gems From the Greek Daily Devotional 1*
Sparkling Gems From the Greek Daily Devotional 2*
Spiritual Weapons To Defeat the Enemy
Ten Guidelines To Help You Achieve
   Your Long-Awaited Promotion!*
365 Days of Power*
Turn Your God-Given Dreams Into Reality*
You Can Get Over It*

*Digital version available for Kindle, Nook, iBook,
and other eBook formats.
**Available only through the iBooks Store.
Note: Books by Rick Renner are available for purchase at:
www.renner.org

The Harrison House Vision

Proclaiming the truth and the power
of the Gospel of Jesus Christ with excellence.
Challenging Christians
to live victoriously,
grow spiritually,
know God intimately.

Harrison House

Connect with us on

Facebook @ **HarrisonHousePublishers**

and Instagram @ **HarrisonHousePublishing**

so you can stay up to date with news

about our books and our authors.

Visit us at **www.harrisonhouse.com**

for a complete product listing as well as

monthly specials for wholesale distribution.